Let's Get Ready for Kindergarten

Strategies, Activities, and Assessments for the Preschool Classroom

Laura Townsend
Illustrated by Bob Masheris

Rigby Best Teachers Press
An imprint of Rigby

Dedication:

In memory of Lois Ackerman who taught me what it was to delight in the smile of a child who loves school and loves her teacher.

To my mom, Judie Krause, preschool teacher for over twenty years. Thanks for sharing with me the many wonderful activities you do with the children in your classroom. They are so lucky to have you as one of their first teachers.

For more information about other books from Rigby Best Teachers Press, please contact Rigby at 1-800-822-8661 or visit **www.rigby.com**

Editor: Pam Gunter
Executive Editor: Georgine Cooper
Designer: Masheris Associates, Inc.
Design Production Manager: Tom Sjoerdsma
Cover Illustrator: Bob Masheris
Cover Photography: Sharron Hoogstraten
Interior Illustrator: Bob Masheris

Text and illustrations copyright © 2002 Rigby
All Rights Reserved.

07 06 05 04 03 02
10 9 8 7 6 5 4 3 2 1

Printed in the United States of America

ISBN 0-7578-2420-X
Let's Get Ready for Kindergarten

Only portions of this book intended for single classroom use and not for resale or distribution may be reproduced without permission in writing from the publisher. Reproduction for an entire school or district is prohibited. Any other use or reproduction of these materials requires the prior written consent of Rigby.

Table of Contents

Introduction	4
Classroom Conditions for Success	6
Social/Emotional Development	10
Oral Language Development	22
Written Language Development	46
Fine Motor Development	88
Large Motor Development	98
Logical/Mathematical Development	116
Parent Activities	154
Scope and Sequence	170
References	175

Introduction

The first day of kindergarten is a highly anticipated event in a child's life. Many of us remember our own first day of kindergarten. The new shoes and clothes are purchased, the backpack is brimming with new school supplies, and the camera is loaded with film. Off go little Johnny and Jennifer on their first day of school.

But questions remain. Are Johnny and Jennifer really ready for that first day of kindergarten? Do they have the necessary skills to be successful in their kindergarten year? How can you, the preschool teacher, help prepare them for the first year of formal schooling?

Indeed, as a preschool teacher, you are the first of many teachers children will encounter. Your job is an awesome one! With the help of this book, you can prepare the children in your preschool class to start kindergarten with the skills they need to be successful.

Preschool is often a child's first separation from home and family. It may also be the child's first structured program, both socially and academically. As a preschool teacher, you will want to make sure that your curriculum covers a broad array of developmental areas. These include: social and emotional development, large and fine motor development, language development—both oral language and written language—and logical and mathematical development. These curriculum areas will be covered in the activities in this book.

How are the activities organized? Each activity lists the main purpose, the areas of development that correlate with the activity, and the materials needed. The area of development listed first provides the main focus of the activity. Each activity also includes ideas for observational notes. *Teacher tips* give you additional suggestions to meet the various needs of the children in your class. Some activities also give you ideas to share with parents and guardians. These are labeled *Home Connection*. Letters are included to give family members additional ways to foster the various developmental areas at home.

Most importantly, as you work on preparing your preschool children for kindergarten, have fun! Help children to see the joy in learning. Treat them with respect and watch them grow as learners.

Classroom Conditions for Success

Brian Cambourne (1988) observed that children need to be engaged to learn. After watching children in the classroom, he discovered several common conditions in classrooms with engaged learners. These conditions are: Immersion, Expectation, Responsibility, Approximation, Demonstration, Use, and Response. As you set up your classroom and plan activities for children, keep these conditions in mind.

Immersion

Children who are immersed in language, both oral and written, will learn naturally. Be sure to encourage plenty of meaningful dialogue in your classroom. In addition, create a print-rich environment. As children enter the classroom, greet them and ask them a question. Vary the questions daily to elicit different responses. Encourage children to share stories about events in their lives. Find time to carry on meaningful conversations with children in small groups and individually.

Immerse children in print by providing them with many books to peruse. Decorate the room with songs and rhymes on charts that children can revisit on their own. Label classroom objects. Write down children's experiences for them. Provide children with daily opportunities to hear and see language.

Expectation

Set expectations for children and let them know what these expectations are. Treat children in a way that shows them that you expect them to learn. The higher your expectations, the harder children will work to meet those expectations. By providing children with opportunities to practice their developing skills, you are setting expectations for them.

Responsibility

Although we can provide many opportunities for children to learn, it is up to each child to take those opportunities and make the most of them. Children are responsible for extracting value from experiences and internalizing it. For instance, when learning how to write her name, Cindy may only attend to the beginning letter at first. For a time, she may practice her uppercase C and scribble the rest of her name. However, continue to model her name for her. Eventually Cindy will take on the responsibility of learning another letter or two. Before long, she will be writing her entire name.

Approximation

Encourage children to try when they encounter something unfamiliar or challenging. Don't expect perfection. As babies, we probably said "D… d …d . . . " for "Daddy" at first. That's approximation! Every parent knows what a little one wants when he or she points to Dad and says, "D …d …d . . . "

When a child "reads" to you a story that he or she has written, congratulate the child on a story well told. Encourage him or her to write more. Point out what a fantastic job he or she did in spelling out the word *dog*.

Encourage approximations in your classroom. Approximations lead to wonderful learning opportunities for children and assessment opportunities for teachers.

Demonstration

Modeling for the children in your classroom should occur on a daily basis. Many of us learn best when we can first observe what we are supposed to learn. For example, I never would have learned to play golf if I hadn't watched my dad swing his club over and over again while he talked me through the motions.

Children need to see you reading and writing and counting. They need to watch a proficient learner work through a task. As you demonstrate for children, explain the process along the way. In other words, share your thought process aloud. This sharing of your thought process while modeling is a key element of the instruction in your classroom.

For example, as you read aloud to children, share the connections you make to the book. Perhaps the main character reminds you of someone you know. Share that thought to model the process of making connections when we read.

When writing a letter, model the process of writing. Explain to children how you write the opening of the letter and then go back and reread what you've written before moving on.

Modeling our thought process for various tasks allows children the "inside scoop." It shows them how to think through a problem, approach a book they are reading, or how to write a letter to a friend or family member. Modeling, or demonstration, is a crucial condition for building success in your classroom.

Use

This is the simple act of practicing. Practice, practice, practice. Be sure to provide children with many opportunities to use what they are learning. If you've just modeled counting, give children an opportunity to practice counting. Give them opportunities to practice counting in different ways. Let them count napkins for snack time or pencils for writing time. Let them count the number of students in the room. Provide children daily opportunities to use what they know and are learning.

Response

It is important to give positive feedback to children. Respond to children and their efforts. Tell them what they did right. Let them know that you have noticed their improvements. Encourage children to respond to each other's work, as well. If a child has drawn a picture that she wants to share with the class, allow her classmates to give her positive feedback.

Answering a child's question is a type of response, too. That child knows if the message got across to you or not when you answer. Be sure to set aside time in your daily schedule for sharing and response.

Social/Emotional Development

Self-Portrait

Purpose: To express understanding of self
Areas of development: Social/emotional, oral language, written language
Materials needed: 8 ½" x 11" drawing paper, crayons

1. Give each of the children a sheet of drawing paper and some crayons. Ask them to draw a picture of themselves on the paper. Remind them to look carefully at what they are wearing and to think about the color of their hair and eyes.
2. As children begin to draw themselves, walk around the room and observe how they react to the task. Note which children immediately get busy, seeming confident of how to portray themselves.
3. As children finish their self-portraits, hold short individual conferences with them. Have them tell you about their pictures. Record their thoughts under their pictures.
4. Label and date pictures, and hang them around the room.

Observations

- Which children accurately portray themselves? Note if eye color and hair color are correct in addition to the correct number of body parts.
- Which children easily talk about their self-portraits? Note the kinds of things they share. This can be a great way to discover what is important to children.

Teacher Tip

Do this activity with children at the beginning of the year and again at the end. Be sure to save beginning-of-the-year portraits. Share these with children after they have drawn their end-of-the-year portraits. Talk about the differences that they notice between the drawings.

Home Connection

Encourage adults at home to take pictures of their children and talk about the pictures with them. You might have adults talk about how the child is alike or different from their siblings or from other family members.

I Have Ten Little Fingers

Purpose: To build self-esteem
Areas of development: Social/emotional, oral language, written language, and logical/mathematical
Materials needed: Chart paper (optional) or an overhead transparency (optional), drawing paper, crayons

1. If you want children to follow along with the written text, copy the traditional rhyme "I Have Ten Little Fingers" (page 13) onto chart paper or duplicate it on an overhead transparency.
2. Teach the rhyme to children. Recite it a few times together, pointing to the body parts mentioned.
3. Ask children to draw pictures of themselves to match the words in the rhyme.

Observations

- Which children are able to identify the body parts mentioned in the rhyme?
- Which children lead the recitation of the rhyme after hearing it repeated it several times?
- Which children follow the lead of others?
- Which children accurately depict the mentioned body parts in their drawings?

Teacher Tip

Call on a volunteer who is able to depict himself or herself accurately in the drawing. Ask that child to share the drawing and point out the various body parts as mentioned in the rhyme.

I Have Ten Little Fingers

(A traditional rhyme)

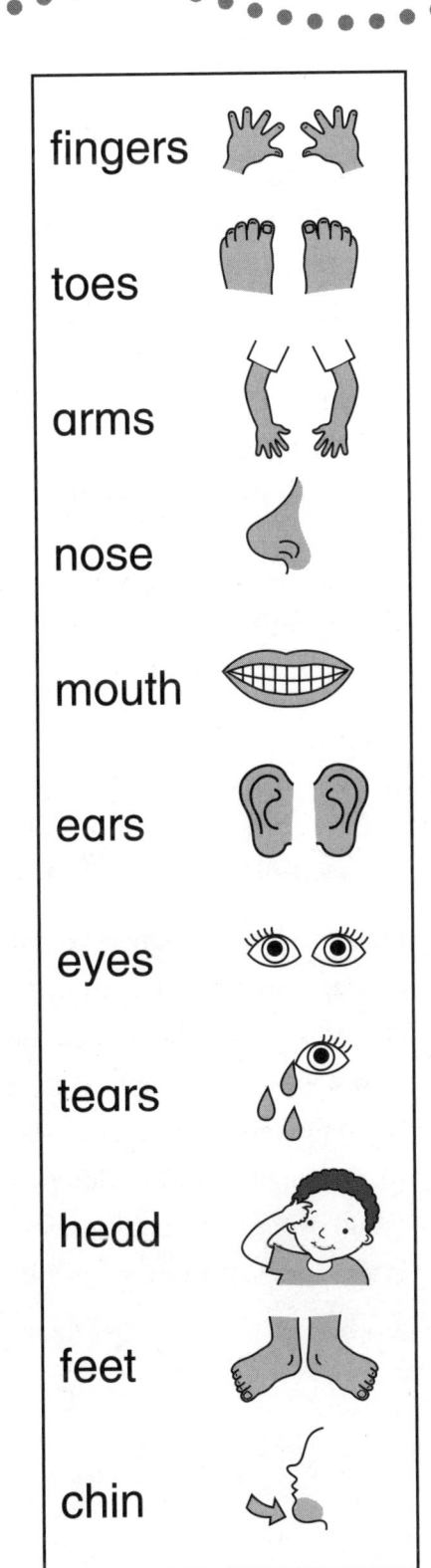

fingers	
toes	
arms	
nose	
mouth	
ears	
eyes	
tears	
head	
feet	
chin	

I have ten little 🖐️🖐️,

Ten little 👣,

Two little 💪,

And one little 👃.

One little 👄,

And two little 👂👂,

Two little 👀

For smiles and 😢.

One little 🧒,

And two little 🦶🦶,

One little 👇 —

That's me complete!

Mary Wore a Red Dress

Purpose: To build self-esteem
Areas of development: Social/emotional, oral language, written language
Materials needed: *Mary Wore a Red Dress and Charlie Wore His Green Sneakers* by Merle Peek, name cards, drawing paper, crayons

1. Make name cards for children in your class.
2. Read the book to children and then teach it as a song. It works well to sing it to the tune of "Mary Had a Little Lamb."
3. Substitute children's names for *Mary* in the song. Hold up name cards, one at a time, to see whom the class will sing about next. Have the selected child identify a piece of clothing he or she is wearing and the color of that piece of clothing. Then sing the new verse together, using that child's name and clothing choice.
4. Have children draw pictures of themselves to match the descriptions in their own verses of the song.
5. Create a class book with these pictures or display them in the room.

Observations

- How did each child react when the class sang about him or her?
- Which children easily recognized their names on the name cards?
- Which children accurately depicted themselves in their drawings?

Teacher Tip

Praise children for their confidence and appropriate behavior when the class sings about them. Note children who appear to act out or shy away when the verse is about them. Be sure to encourage those children to be proud of their names and themselves in an appropriate way.

Partner Pictures

Purpose: To promote and practice cooperation
Areas of development: Social/emotional, fine motor, oral language
Materials needed: 8 ½" x 11" drawing paper, set of crayons per pair of children

Every day we encounter situations where we must cooperate with others. It is never too early to help children learn the valuable life skill of cooperation.

1. Have children work in pairs. Each pair should have one sheet of paper and one set of crayons.
2. Tell children that they will create a picture with their partner. Each partner will draw a part of the picture.
3. Have children decide who will draw first. Tell the child who will draw first: *Draw a yellow sun in the sky.*
4. Tell the child who will draw second: *Draw some green grass on the ground.*
5. Have children continue to take turns drawing, giving the following directions:
   - *Draw a brown tree.*
   - *Now you draw a purple flower.*
   - *Draw a red bird.*
   - *Now you draw an orange butterfly.*
   - *Finish drawing and coloring your picture together.*
6. Have children put their names on their pictures. Hang pictures around the classroom.

Teacher Tip
Be sure to praise those children who negotiate working with their partners especially well. Use their cooperation as a model for other children in the class.

Observations

- Which children easily finish their parts of the drawings and turn responsibility over to their partners?
- Which children are able to negotiate how to finish their pictures?

Pattern Making

Purpose: To promote and practice cooperation
Areas of development: Social/emotional, fine motor, oral language, logical/mathematical
Materials needed: Colored pattern cards, colored plastic cubes or colored paper squares

1. Pair children. Each pair of children should have a colored pattern card and enough colored cubes or colored paper squares to re-create the pattern on the pattern card.
2. Assign each partner a color or two of the pattern.
3. Explain to children that they will work together to create the same pattern on the pattern card using their colored cubes or colored paper squares.

Observations

- Which children are able to work together to re-create the assigned pattern?
- Which children take the leadership role?
- Which children follow?

Teacher Tip

Ask a volunteer to help you complete a pattern. Be sure to share your thoughts with children about how easily they can complete the pattern when they cooperate. Talk about what happens without such cooperation.

Making Colored Pattern Cards

Teacher Directions:

Copy patterns onto heavy cardstock. Color a simple pattern, using two or four colors. Laminate patterns for extra durability.

Cooperative Play Ideas

Purpose: To provide many opportunities to practice cooperative play skills

Areas of development: Social/emotional, logical/mathematical, oral language

Materials needed: A variety of games, puzzles, and building and art materials to provide children with daily experiences to develop their cooperation skills

Use this list of activities to incorporate cooperation into your classroom. Set aside time in your daily schedule for children to practice cooperating. Give children a variety of ways to practice these skills.

- Provide children with building supplies. Encourage them to work with a partner to build something. Building supplies might include: blocks, old boxes, craft sticks, glue, snap-together blocks, and so on.
- Have children role-play various scenarios. Use the cards on page 19 as prompts.
- Allow children to draw a mural for the classroom wall. Encourage each child to add something to the mural.
- Encourage children to do floor puzzles together.
- Have children play card games such as Go Fish!
- Have children play Tic-Tac-Toe with a partner.
- Create a daily or weekly helper board. Assign pairs of children to help with various tasks throughout the day. Encourage partners to work together to complete those tasks. Tasks might include: watering the plants, feeding class pets, passing out snacks, passing out papers or other supplies, choosing a read-aloud story for you to read to the class, and so on.

Teacher Directions:

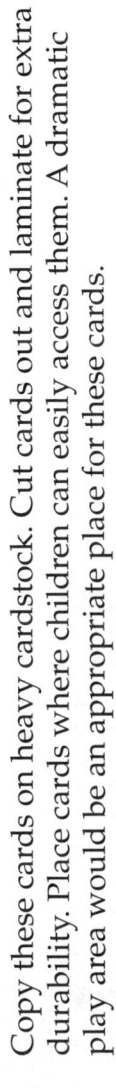

Copy these cards on heavy cardstock. Cut cards out and laminate for extra durability. Place cards where children can easily access them. A dramatic play area would be an appropriate place for these cards.

Role-Playing Cards

© 2002 Rigby

Let's Get Ready for Kindergarten 19

Social/Emotional Checklist

As children engage in some of the activities suggested in this section, or as you observe them throughout the day, note which children exhibit the following behaviors and which do not. Be sure to expose children who are having difficulty with particular behaviors to activities that will help to improve and promote those behaviors.

Social/Emotional Checklist

Name	Engages in cooperative play with others	Engage in dramatic play with others	Shows empathy for others	Displays leadership abilities	Demonstrates the ability to take turns and share	Is willing to take risks	Is willing to attempt new tasks					

Oral Language Development

It's a Mystery!

Purpose: To encourage talk about familiar objects.
Areas of development: Oral language, logical/mathematical
Materials needed: Brown lunch bag, various familiar items that will fit in the bag

1. Show children several objects with which they are familiar, such as a pencil and a key.
2. Ask children to describe each of the objects to you.
3. Then tell children: *I'm going to put one of these objects into the bag. I will give you several clues about the object I put in the bag. Let's see if you can be careful detectives and figure out which object is in the bag.* Be sure to hide the other objects away.
4. Give children several clues about the object such as: *The object I put in the bag is pointed at one end. It is something I use at school. It gets smaller the more I use it.*
5. Gradually increase the number of items you show to children before hiding one. Then begin hiding an object in the bag without showing children any objects beforehand. See if children can guess the contents of the bag with only the clues you give them.

Observations

- Which children express their ideas clearly?
- Which children frequently volunteer to share ideas or guess the contents of the bag?

Home Connection

Send a lunch bag home with children. Ask them to find an object to bring to school in that bag. Have family members talk with children about clues they could give their classmates to help them figure out the mystery object. Share these secret bags as you have time.

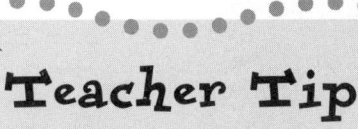

Teacher Tip

Be sure to accept all approximations when children are guessing the contents of the bag. Repeat clues for those children who need to hear clues more than once. Also, ask children from time to time which clues they are using to help them come up with a guess. *Reynaldo, it might be a toothbrush. Which clue helped you to think of that idea?*

Name That

Purpose: To develop children's ability to express their thoughts
Areas of development: Oral language, social/emotional
Materials needed: None

1. Set aside five minutes in your schedule three to five times a week to play a game of Name That.
2. Choose a daily topic and ask children to name objects or ideas that go with the topic. See page 25 for suggestions.
3. As children become more proficient, encourage volunteers to come up with new topics.

Observations

- Which children regularly participate in this game?
- Which children are able to express their thoughts and ideas clearly?

Home Connection

Once a month, send home a list of five topics so children can play Name That with family members.

Teacher Tip

To help children express ideas clearly, model the use of complete sentences. For instance, *Yes, Amanda, a train is a type of transportation.*

Ideas for Name That Topic

- Shapes
- Things to write with
- Body parts
- Types of clothing
- Flowers
- Birds
- Insects
- Computer words
- School supplies
- Furniture found at home
- Furniture found at school
- Transportation
- Pets
- Breakfast foods
- Lunch foods
- Dinner foods
- Girls' names
- Kinds of desserts and cookies
- Places to play
- Toys to play with
- Games to play
- Kinds of cereal
- Ice cream flavors
- Boys' names
- Things to drink
- Sports
- Months
- Days of the week
- Weather words
- Book titles
- Color words
- Numbers
- Letters
- Ways to move from one place to another (hop, jump, and so on)

Riddle This, Riddle That

Purpose: To encourage talk about familiar objects
Areas of development: Oral language, logical/mathematical
Materials needed: Pictures from magazines depicting objects that children can identify or picture cards (See pages 27-29.)

1. Create picture cards as shown on pages 27-29.
2. Show children pictures of two different objects. Then ask them to describe each of the objects. Encourage children to use complete sentences.
3. Once children have described each of the objects, tell them you are thinking about one of the objects. Give children a clue that might help them to guess the object. Continue giving children clues until they are able to identify the object.
4. As children develop their skills in this game, add to the number of pictures children identify and describe at once. You may also extend this game to include objects in the classroom. You may encourage volunteers to think of an object in their heads for the class to try to guess.

Observations

- Which children can express their thoughts clearly as they describe various objects?
- Which children can sort out clues in order to figure out the object in question?

Teacher Tip

As children use complete sentences to express their thoughts, praise them and repeat their thoughts. *Kiana, you are right. A fish does have fins.*

Home Connection

Encourage adults at home to play Riddle This, Riddle That with children. They might create their own sets of pictures using magazines or even family photos.

Teacher Directions:

Copy these picture cards onto heavy cardstock.
Cut them out and laminate them for extra durability.

Picture Cards Set 1

Let's Get Ready for Kindergarten 27

Teacher Directions:

Copy these picture cards onto heavy cardstock. Cut them out and laminate them for extra durability.

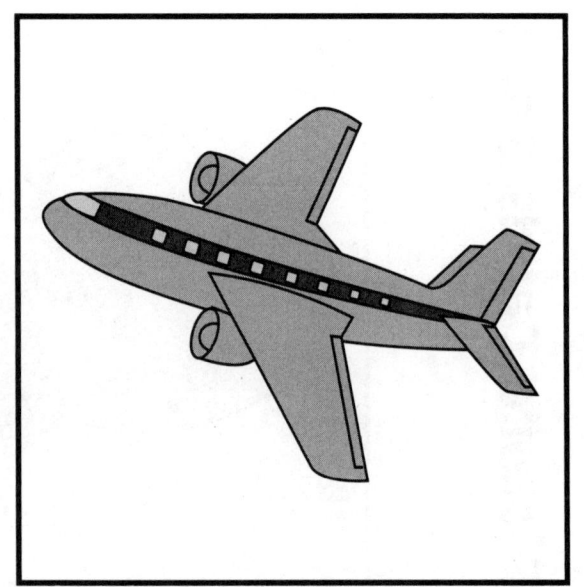

Picture Cards Set 2

28 Rigby Best Teachers Press

© 2002 Rigby

Picture Cards Set 3

Teacher Directions:

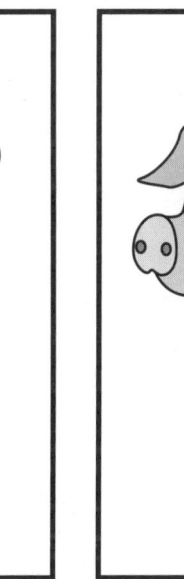

Copy these picture cards onto heavy cardstock. Cut them out and laminate them for extra durability.

Let's Get Ready for Kindergarten 29

What Happened next?

Purpose: To practice oral storytelling
Areas of development: Oral language
Materials needed: None

1. Have children sit in a circle. Tell them that you are going to tell a story together. Explain that this story is going to be told by everyone in the class and even you don't know how it will end.
2. Begin the story by sharing the first sentence: *Yesterday I went to the store.*
3. Have the child sitting next to you add to that beginning. If he or she has difficulty knowing what to say, help with prompts like, *How did I get to the store? What store did I go to? Why did I need to go to the store?* Continue around the circle, giving everyone a turn. If a child struggles to come up with an idea, ask a volunteer to help.
4. Tell a class story often, each time varying the start of the story. You might even suggest the kind of story the class will tell. For instance, *Today let's tell a silly story.*

Teacher Tip

As children develop their story ideas more clearly from one class story to another, be sure to point that out. *Jimmy, I noticed that you didn't need any ideas from me today.*

Observations

- Which children are able to express their ideas clearly and succinctly?
- Which children rely on prompts to help them with ideas?

Home Connection

Encourage adults at home to create family stories around the dinner table or before bedtime. Explain the benefit of oral language development for children.

Story Starters for What Happened Next?

Use any of these story starters as you engage children in What Happened Next?

- On the way home . . .
- Today I'm going to . . .
- We played outside and . . .
- At the zoo, we saw . . .
- When we went to the beach . . .
- We took a trip to . . .
- My pet . . .
- I love to . . .
- One day I saw . . .
- My friends and I . . .
- One day my friends and I were walking through the forest . . .
- My family and I took a trip to . . .
- I wish that . . .
- I laughed so hard when . . .
- At the park I like to . . .

Let's Get Ready for Kindergarten 31

Who? What? Where? When? Why? How?

Purpose: To develop oral language skills used in answering questions
Areas of development: Oral language, social/emotional
Materials needed: Any read aloud story

For children, the ability to answer a question comes with practice. The inverted sentence structure of a question is often confusing for young children, so it is important to model this skill for them.

1. Select a story to share as a read aloud. Before reading, share the title and show the front cover. Then ask children to think about who the characters might be in the story. Tell them that at the end of the story you will want their help in remembering the characters.
2. After reading the story, talk about the story elements in general. *What can you tell me about the story we just read?*
3. Then ask children to remember the characters in the story. *Who are the characters in this story?* If children have difficulty answering this question, model an answer to the question. Model using a complete sentence so children can begin to hear how to change the sentence structure of a question into a statement.
4. Continue to ask questions appropriate to the children's abilities about the story. *What happened in this story? Where did this story take place? When did this story take place? Why do you think that happened? How do you feel about the characters in this story?* If children are not yet ready to answer all of these questions, choose one or more additional W questions to ask. Always highlight a W question before reading the story.

Observations

- Which children can answer questions using correct sentence structure?
- Which children understand the difference between the various questions being asked?

Teacher Tip

Be sure to praise children who use correct sentence structure when answering questions. Repeat the answer for children as a model of correct language structure.

Let's Get Ready for Kindergarten

Then What Happened?

Purpose: To develop understanding of story sequence
Areas of development: Oral language, written language, logical/mathematical
Materials needed: chart paper, tag board or sentence strips, markers

1. Tell children you are going to write a story together. The story can be about a recent classroom visitor, a field trip, or an everyday event. Decide on the topic and write a title for your language experience story on chart paper.
2. Begin the story for the children by writing the first sentence or two on chart paper. Then reread the story to them. For example, *Yesterday we went to the farm. First we saw . . .*
3. Ask for volunteers to give you ideas to complete the next sentence. Then encourage children to retell the experience in the order in which it happened. Be sure to use transition words such as *secondly, next, then, finally.*
4. Once you have finished writing the story for children, reread it together. Emphasize the order in which things happened.
5. Later, write the individual events onto sentence strips. Display the sentence strips in no particular order and read those to children. Ask children for help in putting the story back together again. Remind children of what happened to Humpty Dumpty: *Humpty Dumpty sat on a wall. Humpty Dumpty had a great fall. All the king's horses and all the king's men couldn't put Humpty together again. The same thing has happened to our story. We need to put it back together again.*

6. As children help you reorder the story, be sure to prompt with questions such as: *What happened first? Then what happened? What happened next? What was the last thing to happen in our story?*
7. Once the reordering is finished, read the sentence strips and talk about the order. If an event was misplaced, talk about how that can be fixed.
8. Put the sentence strips and the chart paper story where children can revisit them. Encourage children to reorder the sentence strips on their own.
9. At another time, return to the story with children. Reread the chart paper story.

Observations

- Which children understand the concept of sequencing?
- Which children demonstrate knowledge of transition words?

Teaching Tip

Be sure to emphasize transition words such as *first, second, third, next, then,* and *last.* These words will help children to understand sequencing. You might want volunteers to hold up the cards in order so children can physically see the sequence.

Let's Get Ready for Kindergarten 35

Mistakes

Purpose: To engage children in the oral rhythm of rhyming words
Areas of development: Oral language, written language
Materials needed: Chart paper (optional) or overhead transparency (optional)

1. If you want children to follow along with the written text, copy the traditional rhyme "Mistakes" (page 37) onto chart paper or duplicate it on an overhead transparency.
2. Teach children the rhyme. Recite it together several times.
3. Ask children to listen for the rhyming words. If children do not yet have a good understanding of the rhyming concept, model several examples for them.
4. On chart paper, record pairs of rhyming words children heard. Encourage children to add other rhyming words to the pairs. If the words lend themselves to quick line drawings, add pictures to help children remember what the written words say.

Observations

- Which children are able to identify rhyming words?
- Which children are able to brainstorm additional words to match the rhyming patterns?

Teacher Tip

As children identify rhyming pairs, praise children and say: *You were listening carefully to the last parts of the words.* Repeat the rhyming pairs, saying them slowly so children can hear the rhyming segments.

Mistakes

(A traditional rhyme)

I went upstairs to make my bed;

I made a mistake and bumped my head.

I went downstairs to milk my cow;

I made a mistake and milked a sow.

I went to the kitchen to bake a pie;

I made a mistake and baked a fly.

This Old Man

Purpose: To engage children in the oral rhythm of rhyming words
Areas of development: Oral language, written language
Materials needed: Chart paper (optional) or overhead transparency (optional)

1. If you want children to follow along with the written text, copy the traditional song "This Old Man" (page 39) onto chart paper or duplicate it on an overhead transparency.
2. Teach children the song and the movements that accompany the song. Sing it together several times.
3. Ask children to listen for rhyming words they hear in the song. If necessary, model several rhyming examples.
4. On chart paper, record pairs of rhyming words children heard. Encourage children to add other rhyming words to the pairs. Add quick line drawings to help children remember what the written words say.

Observations

- Which children are able to identify rhyming words?
- Which children are able to brainstorm additional words to match the rhyming patterns in this song?

Teacher Tip

Point out to children that some rhyming words end with the same ending sound. Tell them that this is a strategy they can use to find rhyming words in the books they read. Share some rhyming books that you have previously read.

This Old Man

(A traditional rhyme)

This old man, he played one.

He played knick-knack on my thumb.

Chorus:

With a knick-knack, paddy-whack
(slap your knees twice),

Give the dog a bone.

This old man came rolling home.

Verses:

Two, shoe

Three, knee

Four, door

Five, hive

Six, sticks

Seven, till eleven

Eight, gate

Nine, twine

Ten, once again

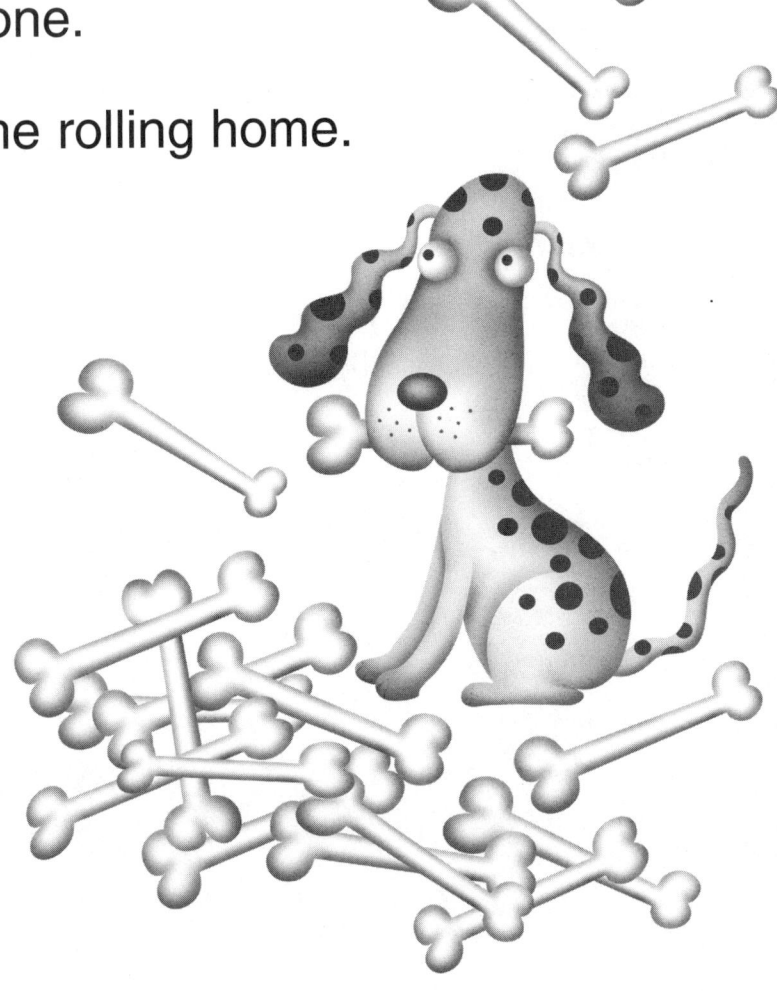

Roses Are Red

Purpose: To engage children in the oral rhythm of rhyming words
Areas of development: Oral language, written language
Materials needed: Chart paper (optional) or an overhead transparency (optional)

1. Copy the traditional poem "Roses are Red" (page 41) onto chart paper or duplicate it on an overhead transparency. You may want to write the rhyming words in another color.
2. Read the poem to children. Then have the children read it with you.
3. As children read the poem again, have them find the pair of rhyming words.
4. Tell children that they are going to create their own version of this poem. Model an example.
5. Together, brainstorm ideas for a new version of this classic. Accept all ideas whether they follow the rhyming pattern or not. If the new version does not rhyme, explain why it doesn't to the children and suggest at least one pair of rhyming words in the poem.
6. Write the poem on chart paper and read it together. Point out rhyming patterns to children.

Teacher Tip

To help children begin the brainstorming process for a new version, you may want to brainstorm words that rhyme with *blue* and *you*.

Observations

- Which children are able to find the pair of rhyming words?
- Which children suggest ideas that follow the rhyming pattern in the original poem?

Home Connection

Copy the class poem for children. Encourage children to decorate their poems and take them home to share with their families.

Roses Are Red

(A traditional rhyme)

Roses are red.

Violets are blue.

Sugar is sweet,

And so are YOU!

Rhyming Card Concentration

Purpose: To develop the ability to recognize rhyming words
Areas of development: Oral language, written language, logical/mathematical
Materials needed: One set of rhyming cards is needed for each small group of children

1. Create rhyming cards using instructions on pages 43-44.
2. Explain the game of Concentration to children.
3. Display the rhyming cards for children to see. Read the words on each card and point out how the pictures on each card match the words.
4. Ask children to find pairs of cards that have words that rhyme. Pair up the rhyming cards together before you send children off to play Concentration on their own.
5. Have children work in small groups to match the rhyming cards. If children need extra support with this task, have them begin with the cards face up. Each child then takes a turn finding a pair of matching cards. Note the symbol on the bottom left-hand corner. This symbol is an additional way to self-check their matches.

Teacher Tip

As children become familiar with the rhyming words in the card set provided, have them help you add cards to the set. They might look through magazines to find rhyming pictures to add.

Observations

- Which children are able to match rhyming words easily?
- Which children rely on classmates or the self-check symbols to make matches?

Rhyming Concentration Cards Set 1

Teacher Directions:
Copy these cards onto heavy cardstock. Cut them out and laminate them for extra durability. Provide one set of cards for each small group of children.

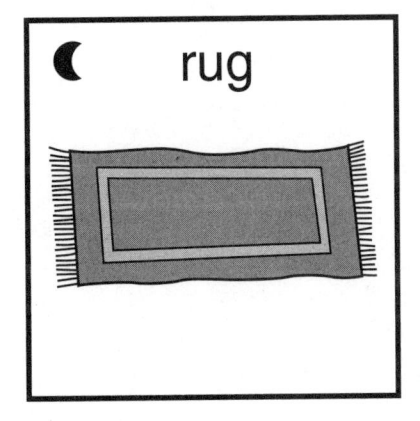

● mop

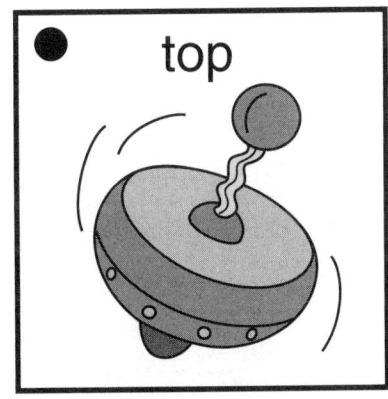

● top

■ tree

■ three

▲ dog

▲ frog

☾ rug

☾ bug

Let's Get Ready for Kindergarten 43

Rhyming Concentration Cards Set 2

Teacher Directions:

Copy these cards onto heavy cardstock. Cut them out and laminate for them extra durability. Provide one set of cards for each small group of children.

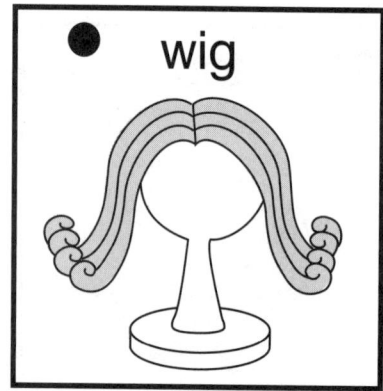

● pig

● wig

■ cat

■ hat

▲ boat

▲ goat

☾ car

☾ star

44 Rigby Best Teachers Press

A, B, C . . . Look What I Can See!

Purpose: To develop the association between letters and their sounds
Areas of development: Oral language, written language, fine motor
Materials needed: 26 pieces of tag board (size dependent on the available wall space), magazines, markers, scissors, glue

1. Create posters for each letter of the alphabet. Label each poster with both an uppercase and lowercase letter.
2. Work with a small group of children. Have them look through magazines and find five pictures of objects that they know. Have them cut out the pictures.
3. Ask children to name the pictures and tell the beginning sound they hear for each picture. Children may give you the letter sound or the letter name. Reinforce either answer while adding the other bit of information. For instance, *Dog does start with /d/ which is what the letter d says.*
4. Have children glue pictures to the correct posters. Label the pictures to show the connection between beginning letters and their corresponding sounds.
5. Hang these alphabet posters around the room. Revisit the posters often. *Who can find a picture on our poster that starts with /l/? Who can find a picture of a ball? What sound does it start with? What letter makes that sound?*

Teacher Tip

For children who have difficulty associating letters and sounds, use classmates' names as prompts for letter/sound associations. For instance, lettuce *starts just like* Laura. *They both start with the /l/ sound. They both start with an l.*

Observations

- Which children can identify the beginning sounds of the pictures they cut out?
- Which children understand the connection between sounds and letters?

Home Connection

Encourage adults at home to make an ABC book with children. Children can cut pictures from magazines for their own books. Suggest that adults take pictures of objects around the house to include in the ABC book.

Written Language Development

We Can Read Our Environment

Purpose: To recognize environmental print
Areas of development: Written language, oral language, fine motor
Materials needed: Examples of environmental print, (Refer to page 49 for ideas.), large drawing paper or heavy tag board

1. Gather examples of environmental print.
2. Post these examples on a bulletin board where children can easily see them.
3. Create a large-sized class book, using drawing paper or heavy tag board. Title the book *We Can Read . . .*
4. Have volunteers glue one example of environmental print onto each page in the book.
5. Under each example, write in large letters, "We can read _____."
6. Read the book with children frequently. Encourage children to read the underlined word using the picture cue. Each reading should focus on a different skill:
   - What letters do you notice?
   - How do you know what this sign, ad, and so on says?
   - How many *m*s or other letters can you find in this book?

Observations

- Which children can read environmental print examples?
- Which children can identify individual letters in the examples?
- Which children recognize the consistent message *"We can read…"* on each page?

Teacher Tip

Model directionality for children as you read the class book. Point to each word as you read so children can follow the process of left to right progression.

Environmental Print Concentration

Purpose: To recognize environmental print
Areas of development: Written language, social/emotional, logical/mathematical
Materials needed: Environmental print cards (See page 49 for directions.)

1. Create environmental print cards as shown on page 49.
2. Work with a small group of children. Place three to five matched pairs of environmental print cards out on a table, right side up.
3. Have children identify each set of cards. Talk about the features of each card. What letters appear in the environmental print? What colors? Any other identifying features such as mascots or icons?
4. Mix up the cards. Place them upside down on the table. Review or teach the game of Concentration to children. Allow the group to play a few rounds with your supervision.
5. Once children are comfortable with three to five sets of pictures, add additional sets.
6. Encourage children to play this game during their free choice time.

Teacher Tip

Have children talk about how they identified various environmental print examples. Point out the different strategies used. Some children may have noticed letters while others may have noticed colors or mascots.

Observations

- Which children can identify individual letters in environmental print examples?
- Which children can read environmental print examples?

Home Connection

Encourage adults at home to read examples of environmental print aloud to children as they are driving in the car. *Look, Mary! That sign says. . .*

Environmental Print Cards

Teacher Directions:

1. Gather coupons, advertisements, cereal and other food box front panels, and photographs of local business signs.
2. Pair up environmental print examples. For instance, a coupon for a type of soup and a label from that same soup can be used to create a pair of environmental print cards.
3. Mount these examples on index cards or heavy tag board cut into 3 ½" x 5" cards.
4. Laminate these cards for extra durability.

Examples of environmental print:

- Fast food restaurant bags and napkins
- Photographs of local grocery store signs
- Photographs of local retail store signs
- Photographs of local gas station signs
- Front panels from food boxes
- Candy bar wrappers
- Newspaper advertisements
- Computer advertisements
- T.V. advertisements

- Soup labels
- Coupons
- Street signs
- Junk mail
- Billboards
- Menus

My Own *I Can Read* . . . books

Purpose: To recognize environmental print
Areas of development: Written language, oral language
Materials needed: Examples of environmental print, magazines, *I Can Read* . . . book for each child

1. Make a copy of the *I Can Read* . . . book, found on pages 51-55, for each child.
2. Have children choose examples of environmental print to glue into their books.
3. Read children's books with them, pausing at the sentence blank on each page.
4. Encourage children to help you fill in the blanks with the letters they hear.
5. Encourage children to read their books to friends.

Observations

- Which children find environmental print examples that they can read?
- Which children give you appropriate names for the sounds they heard while you filled in the blanks of their books?
- Which children were eager to share their books?

Home Connection

Send these books home with children to share.

Teacher Tip

Accept children's approximations as they give you letters to fill in the blanks. Prompt children with familiar words that may help them identify the letters needed.

I Can Read . . . Pages

I Can Read

By _____

I can read _____.

I can read _____.

I can read _____.

I can read _____.

I can read _____.

I can read _____.

I can read _____.

I can read _____.

Let's Get Ready for Kindergarten 55

Environmental Print Hopscotch

Purpose: To recognize environmental print
Areas of development: Written language, large motor, social/emotional
Materials needed: Environmental print cards, masking tape, beanbag, clear plastic tape

1. Create environmental print cards as shown on page 49.
2. Using masking tape, create a Hopscotch grid on the floor. Be sure the boxes are large enough for children to hop into them.
3. Tape an environmental print card in each square. Cover with clear plastic tape for durability.
4. Review with or teach children how to play Hopscotch. (See rules on page 57.)
5. As children hop into each square, have them read the environmental print cards aloud. If children are not able to identify one of the environmental print cards they land on, their turn is over.

Teacher Tip

If some children are having difficulty reading the cards, pair them up with a partner who can help. Note which examples seem easier for children to read and talk about why this is so. Help children understand strategies to identify easier examples. Connect those strategies to ways children can read harder examples.

Observations

- Which children can read environmental print examples?
- Which children can hop easily from one Hopscotch square to another while remaining within the square outlines?

Basic Hopscotch Rules

1. Player 1 tosses the beanbag into square 1.
2. Then player 1 hops over square 1 to square 2. All hopping is done on one foot.
3. Player 1 continues to hop into all the squares and back again.
4. When player 1 reaches square 2 on the way back, he or she stops to pick up the beanbag from square 1.
5. The player then hops into square 1, and out of the Hopscotch grid.
6. Player 1 can continue tossing the beanbag into successive squares until one of the following happens:
   - the player doesn't throw the beanbag into the correct square
   - the player steps on a line
   - the player loses balance when picking up the beanbag or while hopping
   - the player enters a square with the beanbag in it
   - the player puts two feet down in a box
7. When player 1 is finished, player 2 begins.
8. Player 1 starts the next turn where he or she left off.
9. The player to throw the beanbag successfully into every square first is the winner.

Teacher Tip

Rules may need to be modified depending on the gross motor skills of the children playing.

Old MacDonald Had a Farm

Purpose: To help children identify letters of the alphabet
Areas of development: Written language, oral language
Materials needed: Chart paper (optional) or an overhead transparency (optional), index cards

1. Copy the traditional song "Old MacDonald Had a Farm" (page 59) onto chart paper or duplicate it on an overhead transparency.
2. Using index cards, make multiple letter cards with the letters *E*, *I*, and *O* on them.
3. Give each child one of those letter cards.
4. Sing the song together once. Model the use of the letter cards before distributing them to the children. Then ask children to hold up their letter cards when their letters are said aloud. You may want to read the enlarged text slowly so children have time to react when their letter is recited.

Observations

- Which children can recognize their assigned letters, both orally and in the written text?

Teacher Tip

Praise children who hold up their letter cards readily on cue. Ask several children how they determined when it was time to do so. Some children may have been listening for the letter names while others were looking at the written text and matching their letter cards with the text.

Old MacDonald Had a Farm

(A traditional song)

[Old MacDonald] had a [farm], E-I-E-I-O.

And on this [farm] he had some [chicks], E-I-E-I-O.

With a chick-chick here

And a chick-chick there.

Here a chick, there a chick,

Everywhere a chick-chick.

[Old MacDonald] had a [farm], E-I-E-I-O.

Other verses:

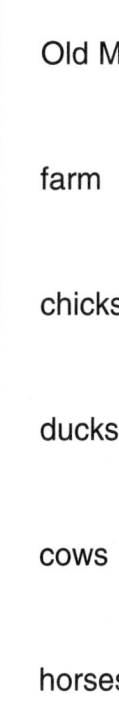

[ducks] : quack-quack

[cows] : moo-moo

[horses] : neigh-neigh

[dogs] : woof-woof

[cats] : meow-meow

[pigs] : oink-oink

[sheep] : baa-baa

Old MacDonald	
farm	
chicks	
ducks	
cows	
horses	
dogs	
cats	
pigs	
sheep	

Let's Get Ready for Kindergarten

Bingo

Purpose: To help children identify letters of the alphabet
Areas of development: Written language, oral language
Materials needed: Chart paper (optional) or an overhead transparency (optional), index cards

1. Copy the traditional song "Bingo" (page 61) onto chart paper or duplicate it on an overhead transparency.
2. Using index cards, make multiple letter cards with the letters *B, I, N, G,* and *O* on them.
3. Give each child one of those letter cards.
4. As you sing this song together, have children hold up their letter cards when their letters are said aloud. You may want to read the enlarged text or sing the song slowly so children have time to react when their letter is recited. Once a child's letter is replaced with a clap, the child keeps his or her letter down.

Observations

- Which children can recognize their assigned letters, both orally and in the written text?

Teacher Tip

As children identify the letters *B, I, N, G,* and *O,* you may want to point out classmates' names that also have those letters in them.

60 Rigby Best Teachers Press

Bingo

(A traditional song)

There was a farmer had a dog

And Bingo was his name-o.

B-I-N-G-O, B-I-N-G-O, B-I-N-G-O,

And Bingo was his name-o.

There was a farmer had a dog

And Bingo was his name-o.

(clap)-I-N-G-O, (clap)-I-N-G-O, (clap)-I-N-G-O,

And Bingo was his name-o.

Note: Leave out one more letter in each subsequent verse.

Miss Mary Mack

Purpose: To help children identify letters of the alphabet
Areas of development: Written language, oral language
Materials needed: Chart paper (optional) or an overhead transparency (optional), index cards or letter cards

1. Copy the traditional rhyme "Miss Mary Mack" (page 63) onto chart paper or duplicate it on an overhead transparency.
2. Make a set of letter cards using index cards or the cards provided on pages 64-67.
3. Give each child a letter of the alphabet.
4. Ask children to look and listen for their assigned letters as you read the rhyme together. Have volunteers match their letter cards with the letters in the rhyme.

Observations

- Which children can match their assigned letters to the correct letters in the rhyme?

Home Connection

Send a copy of this poem home with children. Have adults work with children to find and circle the following high-frequency letters: *b, c, e, f, h, m, s.*

Teacher Tip

Some children will be assigned letters that appear as both uppercase and lowercase letters in the rhyme. Praise children who notice that their assigned letters appear in two different formats in the rhyme.

62 Rigby Best Teachers Press

© 2002 Rigby

Miss Mary Mack

(A traditional rhyme)

Miss Mary Mack, Mack, Mack,

All dressed in black, black, black,

With silver buttons, buttons, buttons,

All down her back, back, back.

She asked her mother, mother, mother,

For fifteen cents, cents, cents,

To see the elephants, elephants, elephants,

Jump over the fence, fence, fence.

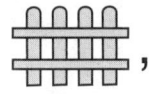

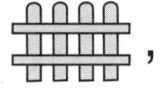

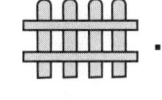

They jumped so high, high, high,

They touched the sky, sky, sky,

And never came back, back, back

'Til the Fourth of July-ly-ly.

black	
buttons	
back	
mother	
cents	
elephants	
fence	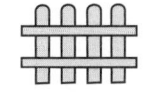
sky	

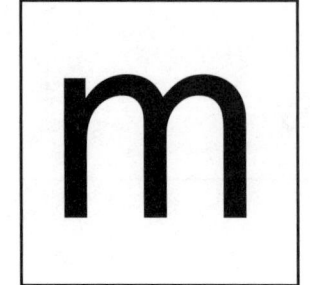

Letter Cards a-m

Teacher Directions:

Copy these cards onto heavy cardstock. Cut them out and laminate for extra durability.

a	b	c	d
e	f	g	h
i	j	k	l
m			

Letter Cards n-z

Teacher Directions:

Copy these cards onto heavy cardstock. Cut them out and laminate for extra durability.

n	o	p	q
r	s	t	u
v	w	x	y
z			

Let's Get Ready for Kindergarten

Letter Cards A-M

Teacher Directions:

Copy these cards onto heavy cardstock. Cut them out and laminate for extra durability.

A	B	C	D
E	F	G	H
I	J	K	L
M			

Letter Cards N-Z

Teacher Directions:

Copy these cards onto heavy cardstock. Cut them out and laminate for extra durability.

N	O	P	Q
R	S	T	U
V	W	X	Y
Z			

Let's Get Ready for Kindergarten

ABC Assessment

Purpose: To assess alphabet knowledge
Areas of development: Written language
Materials needed: ABC Knowledge Assessment card, individual recording sheet for each child, a blank sheet of cardstock

1. Copy the ABC Knowledge Assessment on page 70 on cardstock. Laminate it for extra durability. Make additional copies of the ABC Knowledge Assessment card to use as individual recording sheets for assessing each child's knowledge of the alphabet.
2. Assess the alphabet knowledge of each individual child at the beginning of the year (within the first month of school), at mid-year, and at the end of the year.
3. As you begin work with a child, show him or her the ABC Knowledge Assessment card. Say to the child:
   - *What are these?* Do not use the word *letters*, as you will want to note what the child's response is to these symbols.
   - Cover all but one row of letters at a time with the blank cardstock. This will allow children to focus better. Point to each letter and say: *Tell me what this is.* The following responses are considered correct: the name of the letter, the sound of the letter, or a word that begins with that letter. Note each type of response the child gives you so you can detect any patterns.
   - Continue moving the blank sheet of cardstock down the card, revealing one row at a time.

As children complete this assessment, remember that it is meant to assess their knowledge at that moment in time. Do not use the assessment as a teaching tool at the same time. This assessment will allow you to plan future activities to address the

A, My Name Is Allison

Purpose: To recognize own name and classmates' names; to identify letters of the alphabet

Areas of development: Written language, fine motor, social/emotional

Materials needed: Index cards or sentence strips, storage box, blank paper, writing utensils, photos of the children in your class

1. Write each child's name legibly on an index card or sentence strip. Adhere the child's picture on the back of each card. You may want to laminate these cards for extra durability. Store these cards in a box where children can easily access them.
2. As children have free time, encourage them to find their names in the "Name Box." They can practice reading their names, identifying the letters in their names, and writing their names, using the cards as models.
3. Encourage children to find a partner and practice reading and writing classmates' names together.

Teacher Tip

Note whether a child writes with all uppercase letters, a mix of uppercase and lowercase letters, or correctly with initial uppercase letter followed by lowercase letters. Refer to page 70 for an ABC Knowledge Assessment card.

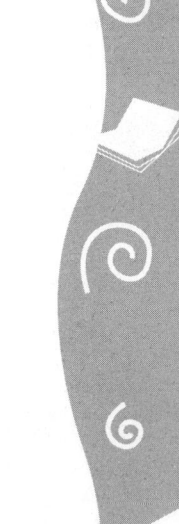

Observations

- Which children can find their names in the "Name Box"?
- Which children demonstrate knowledge of the letter names in their names?
- Which children can recognize classmates' names?
- Which children are able to write their names legibly?

Rooms for Rent

Purpose: To help children identify their own names and the names of their classmates

Areas of development: Written language, oral language, social/emotional

Materials needed: Chart paper (optional) or an overhead transparency (optional), index cards

1. Copy the traditional rhyme "Rooms for Rent" (page 73) onto chart paper or duplicate it on an overhead transparency.
2. Using index cards, make two sets of cards each carrying a child's name. Keep one set for yourself, the other set for the children.
3. Give each child his or her own name card.
4. Before reciting the rhyme together, hold up a name card. Ask the child with that name card to hold it up.
5. Recite the rhyme together, using that child's name to fill in the blank.

Observations

- Which children can easily recognize their own names?
- Which children can recognize the names of classmates?

Teacher Tip

When children easily recognize their names, follow up with this question: *How did you know your name so quickly? What helped you to figure out that this card said your name?* Note what features and strategies children use in identifying their names. Do they notice beginning letters only? Do they notice other letters within their names? Praise children for the strategies used.

72 Rigby Best Teachers Press

Rooms for Rent

(A traditional rhyme)

Rooms for rent,

Inquire within.

When I move out,

Let _____ move in.

Name Concentration

Purpose: To begin recognizing classmates' names
Areas of development: Written language, social/emotional, logical/mathematical
Materials needed: Index cards, photos of the children in your class

1. Take a photograph of each child in your class. Adhere each photograph onto an index card. Print the child's name under his or her photo. These photo cards are set A.
2. On a second set of index cards, write only the names of the children in your class. These name cards are set B.
3. Teach children how to play Name Concentration. First show them several matched pairs of set A and set B cards. Explain to children that they must match a card from set A to a card from set B. Be sure children understand that they can use the names on both the photo cards and the name cards to help them make matches.
4. Allow children to play Name Concentration in small groups. In the beginning, you may want to supervise this process.

Observations

- Which children can match photo cards with name cards?

Home Connection

Encourage adults at home to create their own Name Concentration game, using names of brothers, sisters, parents, other friends or relatives, and even pets.

Teacher Tip

Note the kind of strategies children use to match names. Do they attend to the beginning letters only? Can they match several letters?

My Very Own Rebus Story

Purpose: To develop understanding of word concepts
Areas of development: Written language, social/emotional
Materials needed: 11" x 14" drawing paper, markers, crayons

1. Working with children individually, ask them to dictate a story to you. The story should follow this example: *M my name is[Mark]. I am [5] years old. I like [monkeys].* Ask children to name something they like that begins with the same sound as their first names. The words in brackets will be replaced by pictures that the child draws. For the age of the child, trace the child's hand with the correct number of fingers showing. Write the story for the child, making sure to leave space for pictures.
2. Have children draw pictures of themselves and the things they like in the sentence blanks.
3. Have children reread their stories to you. Encourage children to point to each of the words in their stories. Model this one-to-one correspondence.
4. Collate these stories into a class book. Revisit the book with the class frequently.

Teacher Tip

For children who have difficulty with one-to-one correspondence, have them "hop on" to your finger and read their stories with you. Have children place their pointer finger on top of your pointer finger and read together.

Observations

- Which children know the beginning letters in their names?
- Which children can think of something they like that starts with the same letter as their names?
- Which children can reread their stories to you?
- Which children can point to each of the words in their stories?

Color Concentration

Purpose: To begin to recognize color words
Areas of development: Written language, logical/mathematical
Materials needed: Set of color word concentration cards for each group, a set of crayons for each group (with the color labels still attached to each crayon)

1. Create color concentration cards using the instructions on pages 77-78.
2. Divide children into small groups. Give each group of children a set of color word concentration cards and a set of crayons.
3. Explain the game of Concentration to children. Model how, in this particular game, they can use the crayons to help them read the concentration cards. Also, explain that each card has a picture on it to help children figure out the color words.
4. As children play the game, rotate among the groups, helping those children who need extra guidance. If necessary, join in on a group's game to model the behaviors you are looking for.

Teacher Tip

As children's abilities improve to read the color words, you may want to give each group two sets of the color word cards to play the game Concentration.

Observations

- Which children rely on picture cues or crayons to be able to read the color words?
- Which children quickly read the color words on the cards?
- Which children remember where the matches are when it is their turn to find a match?

Home Connection

Make copies of the cards for children to take home and encourage adults to play this game with them.

Color Concentration Cards set 1

Teacher Directions:

Copy these cards onto heavy cardstock. Cut them out and laminate them for extra durability. You may want to color the pictures before laminating.

yellow

green

blue

red

Let's Get Ready for Kindergarten 77

Color Concentration Cards set 2

Teacher Directions:

Copy these cards onto heavy cardstock. Cut them out and laminate them for extra durability. You may want to color the pictures before laminating.

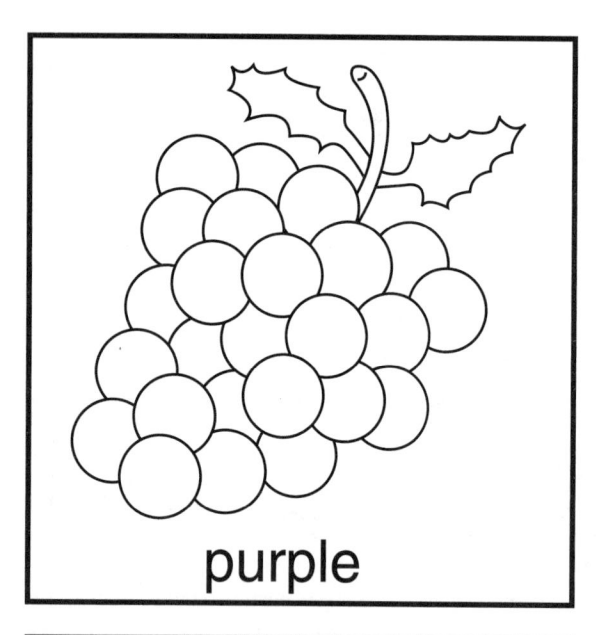

purple

orange

black

brown

78 Rigby Best Teachers Press

© 2002 Rigby

Writing Center

Purpose: To provide opportunities for written expression through letter writing.

Areas of development: Written language, oral language, social/emotional

Materials needed: Writing idea posters from page 80, Writing Center Supplies from page 81

Many children demonstrate a love of writing from a young age. They "write" grocery lists, customer orders as their make-believe restaurants, and letters to parents and friends.

Children generally enjoy engaging in writing activities they have chosen to do more than assigned tasks like writing their names on papers.

By creating a writing center in your classroom, you will be providing the opportunity and materials for children to be immersed in writing frequently.

Teacher Tip

You may want to create a classroom mailbox to encourage children to write to each other.

1. Place writing center supplies from page 81 at a designated writing table.
2. With the whole group, model writing a grocery list from the food list idea poster. See page 80 for instructions. This will allow the children to see the center in action. Ask children to give you names of food that they would like to see on their class grocery list. Write their responses on the paper you have chosen to write on.
3. As children visit the center on their own, encourage them to use the alphabet strip and idea posters to help them spell words.
4. Vary the writing supplies and the posters monthly to stimulate creativity.

Observations

Take time to observe children as they work in the writing center. See the checklist on page 82 to help you with recording observations.

Writing Ideas

Teacher Directions:

Prepare writing idea posters in advance. Each poster should have written words with pictures to match the words. Prepare these on a poster paper so that the children can easily view them. Hang these in your writing center with many writing idea posters. Your poster may look like this:

Grocery List

- apples
- bread
- milk
- hot dogs
- carrots
- bananas
- cereal
- fish

Themes for writing posters:

Family names	Animals
Neighborhood workers	Toys
Things in a park	Things in a house
Body parts	Animals in the ocean
Modes of transportation	Things at a birthday party
Seasonal words	Things on a farm

Writing Center Supplies

- Blank sheets of paper
- Stationary
- Postcards
- Small notepads
- Envelopes
- Alphabet strips
- Stickers that can be used as stamps for letters and postcards
- Clipboards for children to use as a writing surface
- Pre-made books, varying in length from four to ten pages
- Shaped paper to go with a season, holiday, or topic being covered in class (a leaf shape in the fall, and so on.)
- Markers
- Pencils
- Colored pencils
- Crayons
- Stapler*
- Scissors*
- Clear tape*
- Glue*
- Hole punch*
- Yarn*

*These items can be used by children to create their own little books.

Writing Checklist

Name	Uses labels and captions	Retells personal experiences	Writes about personal experiences	Has an awareness of beginning, middle, and end story structure	Writes messages from left to right and from top to bottom	Is willing to take risks	Is willing to attempt new tasks	Phonetically spells words	Correctly forms letters of the alphabet	Uses spacing between letters and words

Concepts About Print

Purpose: To develop children's awareness and understanding of print concepts
Areas of development: Written language
Materials needed: Big Books, pointer, easel

As children begin to explore the meaning of print, not only are they trying to figure out what those symbols (letters and words) say, but they are also trying to understand how print works.

It is important for us to model on a daily basis how print works so children can begin to understand this difficult concept. To us, starting at the left of a page and reading or writing to the right makes perfect sense. In all likelihood, we don't remember a time when print didn't make sense. However, to children who are just beginning to read and write, all the rules of print may be overwhelming and confusing. So set aside time every day to read to children and engage them in meaningful print awareness activities.

1. Display a Big Book (see pages 86-87 for guidance) of your choosing on an easel so children can easily see the book.
2. Engage children in a discussion about the cover of the book.
   - Tell children, as you point with your pointer, that the cover of the book tells us the title, the author, and the illustrator. Briefly explain what an author's and illustrator's roles are if unfamiliar to children.
   - Tell children that the title of the story is always found on the front of a book. You might say: *The title is a clue for us. It tells us how to hold the book the right way as we get ready to read.*
   - As you point to the title, ask children to share their thoughts about the possibilities for this story, such as: *What might this story be about? What clues does the author and illustrator give you through the pictures and the name of the story? So far, does this story remind you of any other stories that you have read?*
3. Next begin a book walk. Walk children through the book. Have a brief discussion about the pictures on each page. Do not read the book to children yet.

4. After talking about the book, go back to the beginning and say: *Now let's read the book and see what happens. Let's find out if some of those story predictions, or guesses, that we made are correct.*
5. As you read the book, point to each word so children can see how you, a proficient reader, navigate through print. Point out one or two of the following print concepts with each visit to the book:
   - We hold the book right side up.
   - We turn one page at a time.
   - We always read the left page before reading the right page.
   - We always begin reading at the left side of the page.
   - We begin at the top of the text and read to the bottom.
   - When we get to the end of a line of text, we move down to the next line.
   - We look at the pictures for ideas of what the words say; the print matches the pictures.

   See the Concepts About Print checklist on page 85 for additional ideas.
6. Return to this Big Book over and over again, each time focusing on a new print concept. As children become familiar with each print concept, ask for volunteers to help you navigate through the book. Ask: *Who can show me where the front cover of the book is? Can you point to the title for me? Where do I begin reading on this page? I've finished reading this page. Now where do I go?*
7. Be sure to leave the Big Book out for children to revisit on their own and with classmates.

Observations

See the checklist on page 85 for observation ideas. Note behaviors during a group reading of the Big Book and those seen during a child's individual time with the Big Book.

Teacher Tip

Work with small groups of children who seem to have difficulty grasping various print concepts. Encourage those children to help you read familiar books together. Be sure to model frequently and praise often when you see desired behavior.

Concepts About Print Checklist

Name	Identifies the front cover	Identifies the title	Demonstrates how to hold a book right side up to read	Demonstrates how to turn pages	Demonstrates where to begin reading on a page	Demonstrates left-to-right movement	Demonstrates top-to-bottom movement	Demonstrates ability to navigate return sweeps (moving from one line to the next)	Demonstrates understanding of a letter	Demonstrates understanding of a word	Demonstrates understanding of one-to-one correspondence	Demonstrates understanding of picture/text match

© 2002 Rigby

Let's Get Ready for Kindergarten

Choosing a Big Book

Big Books are available through many markets today. However, not all Big Books are appropriate for use as a tool in developing concepts about print. Almost any story can be produced in a large format, but only some work well as models for print concepts.

Big Books provide shared reading opportunities for children. These shared reading opportunities are meant to imitate the bedtime story experience for a group of children. (See Don Holdaway's research, 1979, for more information on this.) They also provide opportunities for children to develop understandings about the concepts of print.

How do you choose an appropriate Big Book? Look for the following features:

- The story should be engaging.
- The story should have pictures that match and/or add to the text.
- Children should be familiar with or be able to relate to the story experiences.
- The story language should be natural.
- The characters should be engaging and memorable.
- The text should provide opportunities for children to participate in the reading. This may occur through a recurring phrase, a cumulative text pattern, or through a rhythm and rhyme pattern.
- The ending should satisfy children.
- The amount of text on a page should not be overwhelming to children. You want them to be able to follow along with you as you point to the words.
- The text size should be large enough for children to follow along at a minimal distance.

Once you've chosen a Big Book, have fun reading it with the children. Encourage their participation as you reread the text from day to day. Be sure to keep the Big Book out where children can reread it on their own or with a friend.

Check Out These Big Books!

Barchas, Sarah E. *I Was Walking Down the Road.*
   New York: Scholastic, 1993.

Berger, Melvin. *Growing Pumpkins.*
   New York: Newbridge Communications, Inc., 1994.

Cowley, Joy. *Mrs. Wishy-Washy.*
   San Diego, Ca: Wright Group, 1984.

Fox, Mem. *Hattie and the Fox.*
   Englewood Cliffs, N.J.: Bradbury Press, 1988.

Guarino, Deborah. *Is Your Mama a Llama?*
   New York: Scholastic, 1989.

Hutchens, Pat. *Rosie's Walk.*
   New York: Macmillan, 1968.

Joose, Barbara M. *Mama, Do You Love Me?*
   New York: Scholastic, 1991.

Jorgensen, Gail. *Beware.*
   Crystal Lake, IL: Rigby, 1988.

Jorgensen, Gail. *Crocodile Beat.*
   Crystal Lake, IL: Rigby, 1988.

Martin, Jr., Bill *Brown Bear, Brown Bear.*
   New York: Henry Holt, 1983.

Nayer, Judie. *My Five Senses: A Lion's Tale.*
   New York: Newbridge Communications, Inc., 1994.

O'Brien, Anne Sibley. *Rainy City Rainbow.*
   New York: Newbridge Communications, Inc., 1993.

Parkes, Brenda. *The Enormous Watermelon.*
   Crystal Lake, IL: Rigby, 1986.

Parkes, Brenda. *Kakadu Jack.*
   Crystal Lake, IL: Rigby, 2000.

Parkes, Brenda. *Who's in the Shed?*
   Crystal Lake, IL: Rigby, 1986.

Titherington, Jeanne. *Pumpkin Pumpkin.*
   New York: Scholastic, 1986.

Woody. *I Want My Mom.*
   Crystal Lake, IL: Rigby, 2000.

Fine Motor Development

Amazing Mazes

Purpose: To develop children's motor planning
Areas of development: Fine motor
Materials needed: Copies of a maze, pencils

1. Select one of the mazes from pages 90-92 to copy and distribute to children.
2. Model for children how to follow the maze first with their fingers. Then show them how to use a pencil to complete the maze.
3. Give children copies of a maze. Have them follow the maze, first with their fingers and then with pencils.

Observations

- Which children can plan their pencil movements through the maze?
- Which children can keep their pencil lines within the maze lines?

Teacher Tip

Throughout the year, give children an opportunity to complete the same maze. Note how quickly children can make their way through the maze. Also note how well they are able to keep their pencil lines within the maze lines.

Amazing Maze 1

Teacher Direction:

Copy this maze for children with emerging fine motor skills. Have them follow it first with their fingers and then with a pencil. You may want to laminate the mazes and show children how to use wipe-off markers.

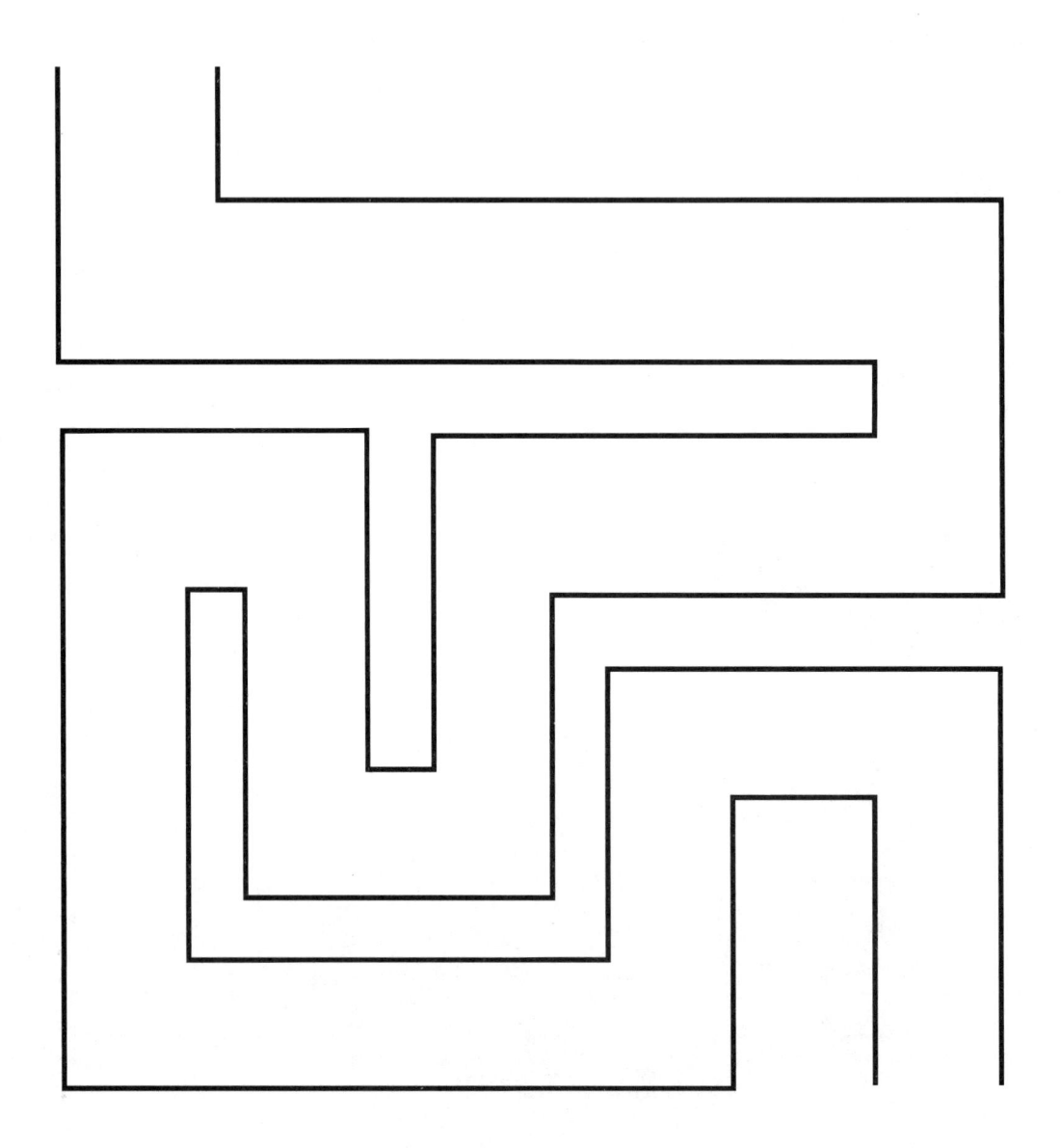

Amazing Maze 2

Teacher Direction:

Copy this maze for children with developing fine motor skills. Have them follow it first with their fingers and then with a pencil. You may want to laminate the mazes and show children how to use wipe-off markers.

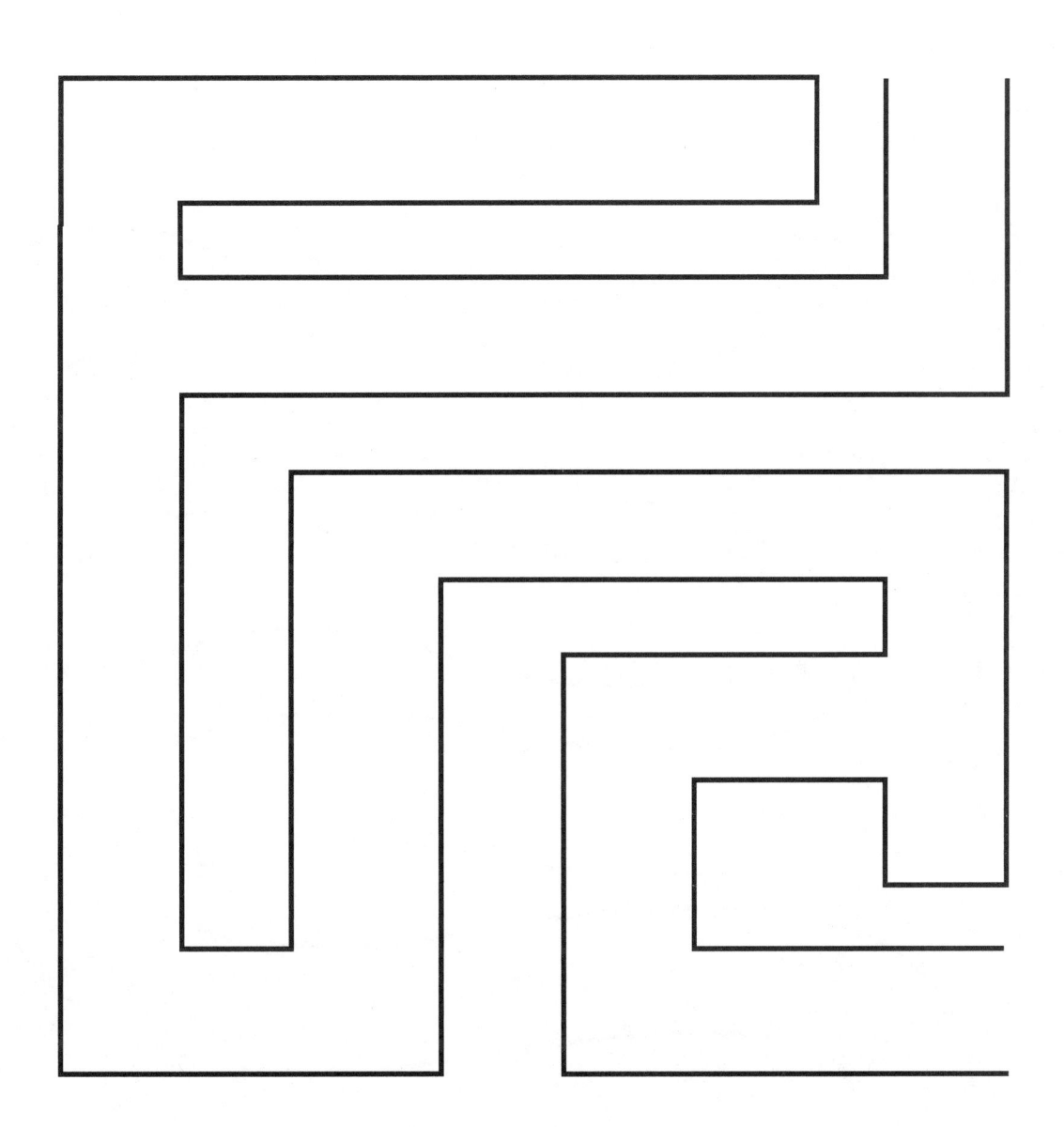

Amazing Maze 3

Teacher Direction:

Copy this maze for children with well-developed fine motor skills. Have them follow it first with their fingers and then with a pencil. You may want to laminate the mazes and show children how to use wipe-off markers.

Fun with Lines and Shapes

Purpose: To develop fine motor movements used in letter writing
Areas of development: Fine motor
Materials needed: Crayons or markers, copies of shape pictures

As children begin to develop fine motor skills for writing legible letters and numbers, provide them with additional opportunities to practice the hand movements they will use when writing.

The following lines and shapes are precursors to letter and number writing:

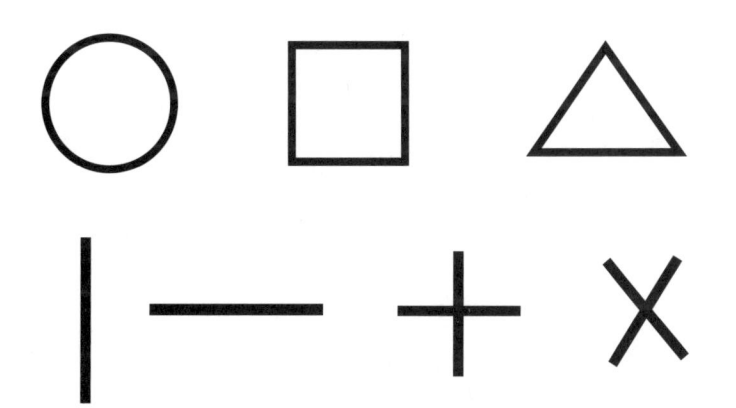

○ □ △

| — + ✕

Teacher Tip
Pull children who are having difficulty with similar shapes together into a small group. Provide them with a different medium such as shaving cream or sand in which to practice tracing the difficult line or shape in.

1. Make a copy of one of the blackline master shape pictures on pages 94-96 for each child.
2. Explain to children that they will use crayons or markers to trace the pictures. Model this for children.
3. Give each child a copy of the shape picture you have chosen. As children work on tracing the picture, walk around and provide help to those children who need it, or take time to observe the fine motor development of children.

Observations

- Which shapes can children trace easily?
- Which shapes provide more challenges for children?

Lines and Shapes Picture 1

Teacher Directions:

Have children trace the line drawing with a crayon or marker so they can see which lines they have already traced.

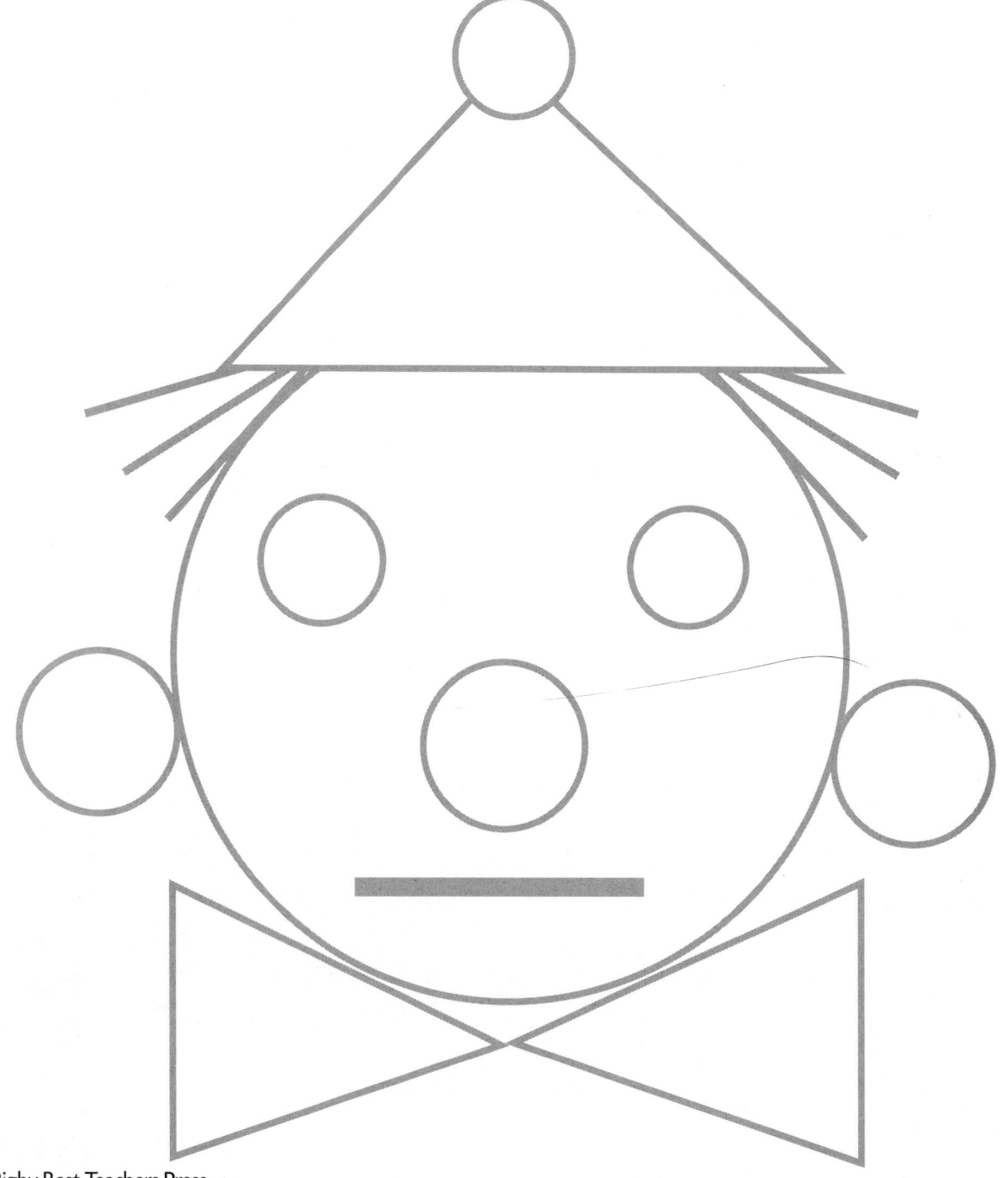

94 Rigby Best Teachers Press

© 2002 Rigby

Lines and Shapes Picture 2

Teacher Directions:

Have children trace the line drawing with a crayon or marker so they can see which lines they have already traced.

Let's Get Ready for Kindergarten 95

Lines and Shapes Picture 3

Teacher Directions:

Have children trace the line drawing with a crayon or marker so they can see which lines they have already traced.

Highlight That!

Purpose: To provide children with correct models of their names while developing fine motor skills
Areas of development: Fine motor, social/emotional
Materials needed: 4" x 6" index cards, highlighter, contact paper or laminate, write-on/wipe-off markers

Have you ever created name cards with dotted lines for children to trace? Did some children imitate that format and use those same dotted lines when writing their names on their own? When a highlighter is used to write children's names, children are able to see the lines they are to follow while at the same time seeing a correct and complete model of their name.

1. Write each child's name with a highlighter on an index card. Laminate each card.
2. Have children use write-on/wipe-off markers to trace their names on their cards. Encourage them to practice their names several times.
3. Place these laminated cards in a box where children can access them during free choice time.

> **Teacher Tip**
>
> Note the level of difficulty children have when they first practice tracing their names. Each time they try this activity, note the level of improvement. Be sure to point out that improvement to individuals. Be specific. For example: *Brad, I noticed that you wrote your d correctly today. You made the ball go in the right direction. Great job!.*

Observations

- Which children can stay on the highlighted lines as they trace their names?
- Which children write their names easily?

Home Connection

Tell adults at home to write their children's names with highlighters. Children can then practice this skill at home.

Large Motor Development

Follow the Leader

Purpose: To develop large motor skills
Areas of development: Large motor, social/emotional, oral language
Materials needed: None

1. Have children line up single file behind you. Tell them to follow you.
2. Begin the game by saying: *Follow the leader. I'm walking.* Then make sure children follow the directions before you change the action. Each time you change actions make sure to say: *Follow the leader. I'm. . .* This will allow children to hear the directions in addition to seeing them.
3. Change actions to skip, jump, hop, march, run in place, walk in a heel-toe pattern, walk on tiptoes, stomp, and so on. Eventually add arm actions.
4. Choose a child to become the leader after a short time.

Teacher Tip

Note which actions are more difficult for children to imitate. Be sure to revisit those actions at other times during the day. For instance, if marching is difficult for children, you might have them march to get their coats or march to go outside to play.

Observations

- Which children can transition easily from one action to another?

Simon Says

Purpose: To develop large motor skills
Areas of development: Large motor, social/emotional, oral language
Materials needed: None

1. Explain the game of Simon Says to children. Tell them: *I will ask you to do different things. But you should only do them if I first say "Simon says." If I don't say "Simon says," then keep doing what you have been doing. If you are caught doing something Simon did not say to do, you will have to sit down.*
2. Begin the game by saying: *Simon says to march in place.* Continue the game. Be sure to say *Simon says* often during the first game.
3. After five sets of directions, choose a new Simon to lead the class.

Teacher Tip

Be sure to praise children as they correctly demonstrate an action or follow Simon's directions carefully. *Susan, you were hopping in place just like Simon said. Good for you!*

Observations

- Which children can demonstrate the physical actions asked of them?
- Which children can quickly transition from one kind of action to another?

Busting out with Balloons

Purpose: To develop upper body motor skills
Areas of development: Large motor, social/emotional
Materials needed: One balloon for each pair of children

1. Blow up balloons.
2. Pair children.
3. Have children work with their partners to keep their balloons in the air by batting them up with their hands. Encourage children to bat their balloons gently so the balloons remain close to them. At first children may find it fun to bat the balloons as hard as they can, but they will come to realize the more gently they bat their balloons, the longer they will be able to keep them in the air.
4. As their balloons fall to the ground, the pair must sit down. The pair who keeps their balloon up in the air longest is the winner.

Observations

- Which children demonstrate motor control as they bat their balloons?

Teacher Tip

Model the difference between batting the balloon gently and roughly or choose a volunteer who has successfully kept his or her balloon in the air to demonstrate for the rest of the class.

Let's Get Ready for Kindergarten

Beanbag Toss

Purpose: To develop upper body motor skills
Areas of development: Large motor, logical/mathematical
Materials needed: Beanbags, large cardboard boxes, counters of some sort (buttons, beads, pennies, and so on)

1. Set up several large cardboard boxes in a line. Assign the box closest to the throwing line one point, the next box two points, and so on.
2. Have children take turns tossing a beanbag into each box, starting with the closest box. If a child tosses the beanbag into the box, he or she gets to count out counters to equal the points assigned to that box. Each child continues to toss the beanbag until he or she misses. Then another child takes a turn.
3. After all children in the group have had a chance to toss the beanbag, have everyone count their counters. Encourage children to remember their point totals and try to surpass that number when they toss the beanbag again.

Observations

- Which children can toss the beanbag accurately into the boxes?

Teacher Tip

Move the boxes closer to those children who are having difficulty tossing the beanbag into even the closest box. For those children who are able to toss the beanbag into the farthest box, move the boxes farther away.

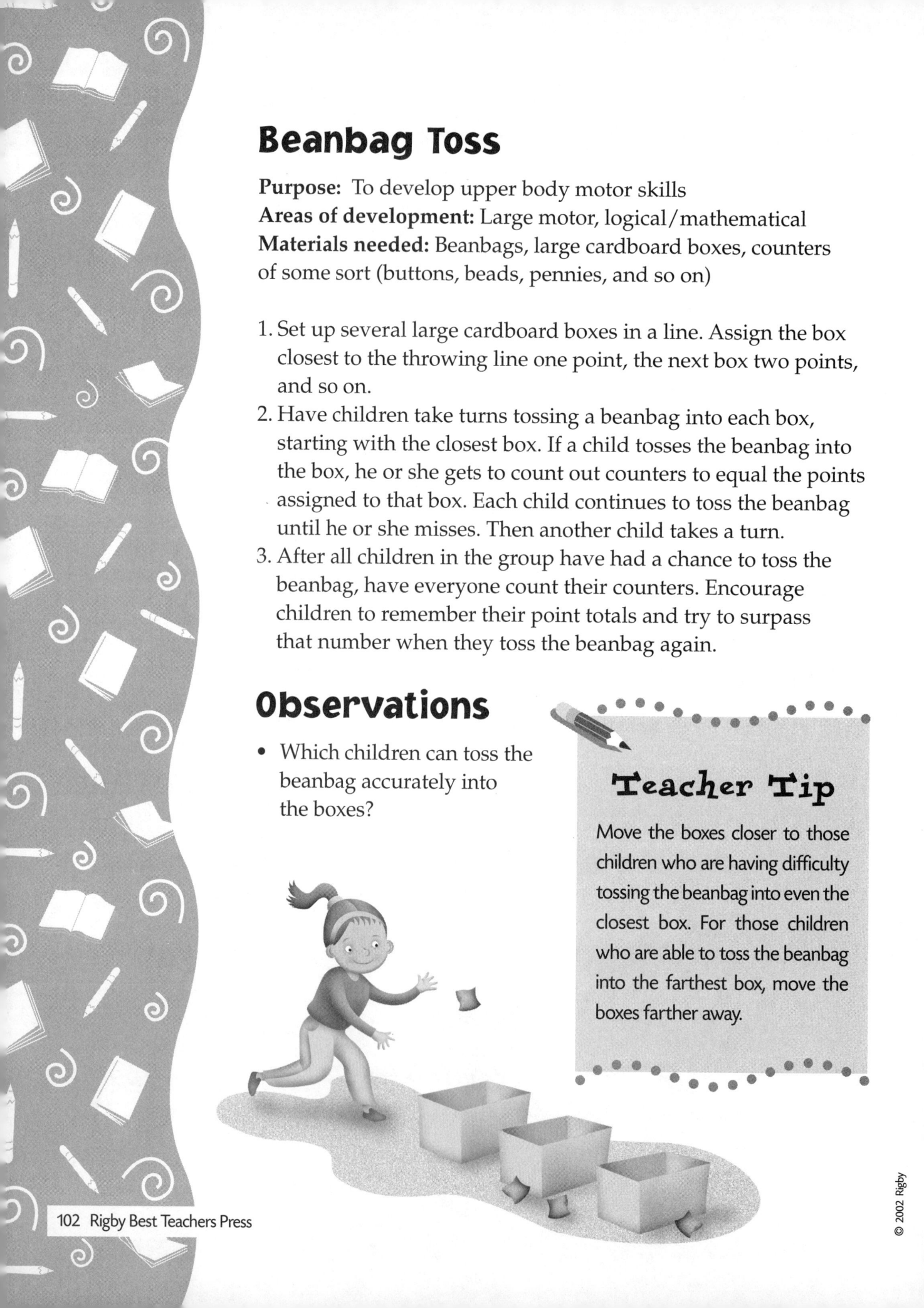

Bowl Me Over!

Purpose: To develop large motor muscles
Areas of development: Large motor, social/emotional, logical/mathematical
Materials needed: Playground ball, empty milk cartons (quart size works best), sand, masking tape

1. Pour a little bit of sand into the bottoms of the milk cartons. Be sure that the sand does not make the milk cartons too heavy. You want children to be able to knock them over, but not too easily.
2. Set up the milk cartons like bowling pins.
3. Draw a line on the floor with masking tape for children to stand behind when they bowl.
4. Model for children how to roll the ball on the floor to knock the pins over.
5. Have children take turns bowling with a partner. The child who is not bowling can count the number of pins the bowler knocks down.

Teacher Tip

As children become better bowlers, you may want to move the line back or add more weight to the milk cartons.

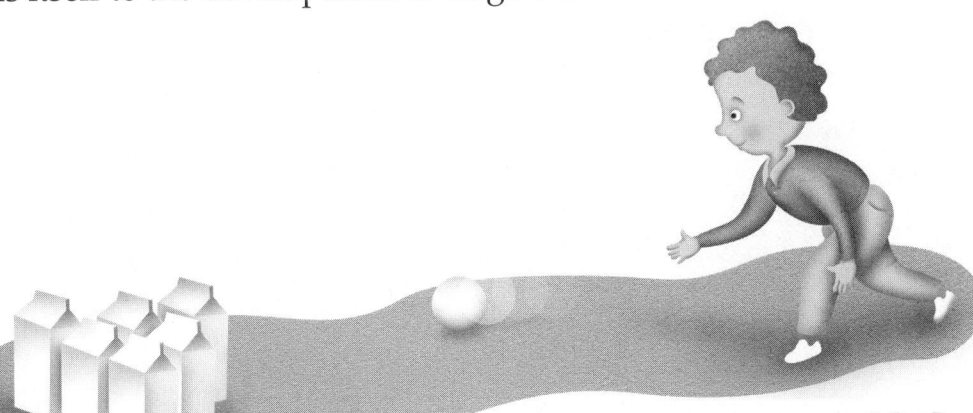

Observations

- Which children can roll the ball accurately to knock down "pins"?

Home Connection

Encourage adults at home to check out Bumper Bowling at their local bowling alleys. Not only is this a fun family activity, but it lends itself to the development of large motor muscles.

Obstacle Course

Purpose: To develop large motor skills
Areas of development: Large motor, social/emotional
Materials needed: Tables, large cardboard boxes, blankets, ropes, masking tape, large building blocks

1. Using a variety of materials, create an obstacle course in a corner of your room.
   - Cover a table with a blanket to create a tunnel.
   - Open up two sides of a large cardboard box to create another tunnel.
   - Lay a rope on the floor in the shape of a circle.
   - Create large stepping stone outlines on the floor with masking tape.
   - Lay out large building blocks for children to step over. Put them in piles of one or two blocks high.
2. Model navigating the obstacle course for children.
3. Encourage children to take turns going through the course with a friend. While one child waits to go through the course, he or she may count how many seconds it takes for his or her partner to go through the obstacle course.

Observations

- Which children can navigate through the obstacle course with ease?
- Which areas appear to be easier for children?

Teacher Tip

Be sure to help those children who have difficulty with the obstacle course by giving them tips on how to navigate through it. If necessary, modify the course to ensure a successful experience.

Let's Get Ready for Kindergarten 105

Head and Shoulders, Knees and Toes

Purpose: To encourage use of large muscles
Areas of development: Large motor development, oral language, written language
Materials needed: Chart paper (optional) or overhead transparency (optional)

1. If you want children to follow along with the written text, copy the traditional song "Head and Shoulders, Knees and Toes" (page 107) onto chart paper or duplicate it on an overhead transparency.
2. Teach children the song and recite it once or twice without movements.
3. Teach children the actions that go with the song. Have children place their hands on their head, shoulders, knees, and toes when indicated in to the song.

Observations

- Which children can easily follow the large motor motions?
- Which children identify the various body parts correctly when mentioned in the song?

Teacher Tip

Ask for volunteers to demonstrate the correct actions to go with the song as the class recites the song slowly.

Head and Shoulders, Knees and Toes

(A traditional song)

Head, shoulders, knees and toes, knees and toes,

Head, shoulders, knees and toes, knees and toes,

Eyes and ears and mouth and nose,

Head, shoulders, knees and toes, knees and toes.

If You're Happy . . .

Purpose: To practice various motions that use large motor muscles
Areas of development: Large motor development, oral language, written language
Materials needed: Chart paper (optional) or overhead transparency (optional)

1. If you want children to follow along with the written text, copy the traditional song "If You're Happy . . ." (page 109) onto chart paper or duplicate it on an overhead transparency.
2. Teach children the first verse of the song along with the motions.
3. Continue singing the song, using the suggested verses or verses suggested by children.

Observations

- Which children demonstrate the motions mentioned in the verses?
- Which children suggest new verses that express other movement?
- Use the large motor checklist on page 115 to note children's accomplishments in this developmental area.

Teacher Tip

If children seem to have difficulty completing the actions for new verses, be sure to have volunteers model the desired action before singing each new verse.

If You're Happy...

(A traditional song)

happy   clap your hands   face

If you're happy and you know it, clap your hands!

If you're happy and you know it, clap your hands!

If you're happy and you know it,

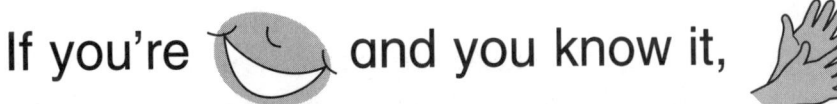

Then your face will surely show it.

If you're happy and you know it, clap your hands!

Other verses:

Stomp your feet

Snap your fingers

Pat your head

Rub your tummy

Shout "Yahoo!"

The Grasshopper

Purpose: To act out the large motor movements
Areas of development: Large motor development, oral language, written language
Materials needed: Chart paper (optional) or overhead transparency (optional)

1. If you want children to follow along with the written text, copy the traditional poem "The Grasshopper" (page 111) onto chart paper or duplicate it on an overhead transparency.
2. Teach children the poem without any physical motions.
3. Recite the poem together, acting out the motion of jumping.
4. Share another version of the poem with children acting out the new movement.
5. Encourage the class to help you write additional versions of this poem, each version incorporating a new motion.

Observations

- Which children successfully demonstrate the various physical motions of jumping, hopping, and so on?
- Use the large motor checklist on page 115 to note children's accomplishments in this developmental area.

Teacher Tip

Model various motions for children. Work in small groups with those who have difficulty with particular motions.

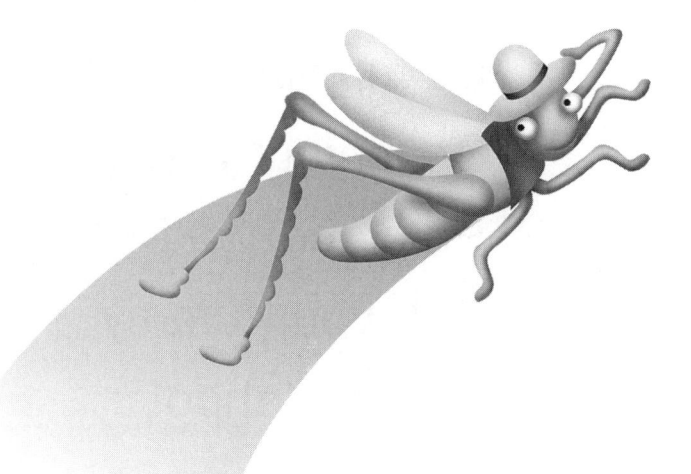

The Grasshopper

(A traditional poem)

There was a little grasshopper

Who was always on the jump.

And because he never looked ahead,

He always got a bump.

Try this next version of the poem
or make up your own.
(Adapted by Laura Townsend)

There was a little grasshopper

Who was always on the hop,

And because he never looked ahead,

He always got a pop.

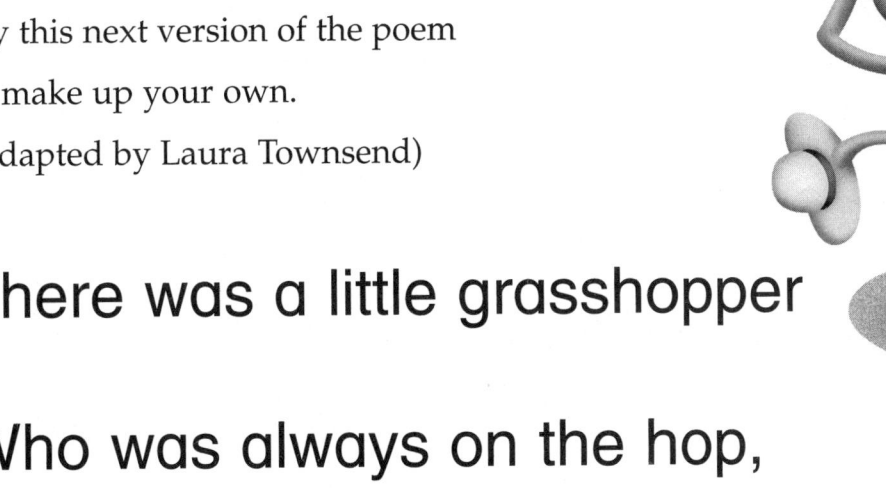

Large Motor Center

Purpose: To provide a variety of activities for development of large motor skills
Areas of development: Large motor, social/emotional
Materials needed: Variety of building blocks, balls, and playthings as listed below.

It is important to provide children with daily experiences to develop their large motor skills. Below is a list of activities and materials that you can use to create a large motor center. Be sure to set aside time in your daily schedule for children to visit the large motor center. Also, be sure to rotate activities so children have the opportunity to use different large motor skills and muscles.

- Have children bounce playground balls back and forth to a partner. Encourage them to work within the space provided and to keep the ball in control.
- Have children practice jumping rope. Children may jump rope by themselves or they may work in groups of three: two children hold the rope between themselves while the third child jumps over the rope. Tell children that they must keep the rope below knee-level for safety reasons.
- Have children play Hopscotch.
- Have children build with large building blocks.
- Have children climb on monkey bars.
- Have children roll on a padded floor or on the ground that has been cleared of debris.
- Have children walk in various ways: tiptoe, march, hop, skip, crawl, crab walk, and so on.

- Have children scoot on a scooter or on their stomachs through a maze built with blocks.
- Have children throw a foam basketball or football to a partner or through a hoop.
- Have children push large cars and trucks around a village that they have created with building blocks.
- Have children push playground balls to a partner on the floor. Create a goal with blocks and have children push the ball through it from a short distance away.
- Have children imitate the movements of various animals.
- Have children play Hokey Pokey.
- Have children play Leapfrog.
- Have children play Duck-Duck-Goose.
- Have children play Freeze!
- Have children bounce tennis balls, racquetballs, and basketballs against a wall.
- Have children practice walking on stilts. You can make these easily with a coffee can by punching holes in the sides and stringing some rope through the holes.
- Have children play Cup Toss. Each child is given a plastic cup. Pairs of children toss a tennis ball back and forth, catching the tennis ball in the plastic cup.

Large Motor Checklist

Use this checklist to assess children's large motor abilities. Assessment can be done on the playground or in the classroom. Encourage children to demonstrate some of these skills games like Simon Says or Mother May I? Assess children throughout the year, at least a minimum of three times— at the beginning, middle, and at the end of the year.

Large Motor Checklist

Name	Stands on one foot 10 seconds without losing balance	Walks toe-heel forward	Walks backward	Runs smoothly	Skips	Gallops	Changes speeds while running, including starting and stopping	Jumps up to 12" without falling	Jumps over objects that are up to 6" high without falling	Hops on one foot	Climbs up and down stairs, alternating feet	Demonstrates understanding of picture/text match	Catches a ball with hands	Throws a ball overhand	Bounces a ball and catches it

© 2002 Rigby

Let's Get Ready for Kindergarten

Logical/Mathematical Development

Vital Information

Purpose: To recognize and retell phone numbers and addresses
Areas of development: Logical/mathematical, social/emotional
Materials needed: One set of number cards or magnetic numbers for each small group, list of children's phone numbers and addresses, index cards

1. Create a set of number cards as shown on pages 128-129.
2. Explain to children the importance of knowing their phone numbers and addresses. Assure them that you understand that many numbers are involved and that you will help them to remember all of these numbers.
3. Write each child's phone number on an index card. On another index card, write his or her address. Pass out the phone number card to children.
4. Divide children into small groups of three or four. Provide each group with one set of number cards or magnetic numbers.
5. Have children take turns reading their phone numbers to their group members. Then have children duplicate their phone numbers using the number cards or magnetic numbers. Children can help each other check their phone numbers.
6. As children become more acquainted with their phone numbers and addresses, pairs of children can "quiz" each other using cards.

Observations

- Which children are able to identify the numbers in their phone numbers and addresses?
- Which children can recognize and retell their phone numbers and addresses?

Home Connection

Encourage adults at home to work with children to learn their addresses and phone numbers. Suggest that children push the buttons on the telephone (with parent supervision) to learn how to dial home when visiting friends or relatives.

Teacher Tip

Provide play telephones and envelopes for children to practice their telephone numbers and addresses.

Over in the Meadow

Purpose: To practice counting

Areas of development: Logical/mathematical, written language, oral language, fine motor

Materials needed: Chart paper (optional) or overhead transparency (optional), drawing paper, crayons or markers

1. If you want children to follow along with the written text, copy the traditional rhyme "Over in the Meadow" (page 119) onto chart paper or duplicate it on an overhead transparency.
2. Read the rhyme to children. Then encourage them to read it with you.
3. Ask children to help you make new verses by changing the animals and the sounds they represent. Write these out so children can see their suggestions in print.
4. Reread the rhyme with children, including the new verses.
5. Give children drawing paper and some crayons or markers. Ask them to draw a picture to go with one of the verses.

Observations

- Which children draw pictures that correctly match a verse?

Teacher Tip

Encourage children to count the animals in their pictures aloud for you.

Over in the Meadow

(A traditional rhyme)

Over in the meadow
In the sand, in the sun,
Lived an old mother toadie
And her little toadie one.
"Croak!" said the mother.
"I croak!" said the one.
So they croaked and they croaked
In the sand, in the sun.

Over in the meadow
In the stream so blue,
Lived an old mother fishie
And her little fishies two.
"Swim!" said the mother.
"We swim!" said the two.
So they swam and they swam
In the stream so blue.

Note: Continue on with your own rhymes, each time adding to the number of little ones in the meadow.

Hickory Dickory Dock

Purpose: To practice counting, number sense
Areas of development: Logical/mathematical, oral language, written language
Materials needed: Chart paper (optional) or overhead transparency (optional), index cards or number cards

1. If you want children to follow along with the written text, copy the traditional rhyme "Hickory Dickory Dock" (page 121) onto chart paper or duplicate it on an overhead transparency.
2. Write numbers on index cards or use the number cards provided on page 128. Give each child a number.
3. Recite the rhyme with children. Ask children to listen for the number they are holding. If they hear it they should hold up their number. To further develop their number awareness, have children exchange their numbers as the verse is repeated.

Observations

- Which children can identify their assigned numbers and recognize those same numbers in the rhyme?
- Which children can transition from one recitation of the rhyme with one number to another recitation of the rhyme with a new number?

Teacher Tip

Praise children who display their numbers as they are mentioned in the rhyme.

120 Rigby Best Teachers Press

© 2002 Rigby

Hickory Dickory Dock

(A traditional rhyme)

Hickory dickory dock,

The mouse ran up the clock.

The clock struck one.

The mouse ran down.

Hickory dickory dock.

Hickory dickory dock,

The mouse ran up the clock.

The clock struck two.

The mouse ran down.

Hickory dickory dock.

Elephant Song

Purpose: To practice counting
Areas of development: Logical/mathematical, oral language, written language, large motor
Materials needed: Chart paper (optional) or overhead transparency (optional)

1. If you want children to follow along with the written text, copy the traditional rhyme "Elephant Song" (page 123) onto chart paper or duplicate it on an overhead transparency.
2. As you recite the rhyme with children, have them clap their hands or stomp their feet to correspond with the numbers in the rhyme.

Observations

- Which children demonstrate an understanding of the correlation between the numbers in the rhyme and the number of times they clap or stomp?
- Which children can continue the counting pattern in the rhyme?

Teacher Tip

Ask volunteers to draw pictures of elephants. Then, using the number cards on pages 128-129 and the elephant pictures along with a pocket chart or flannel board, have children put a number in front of the elephants to correspond to the number of elephants in the rhyme.

Elephant Song

(A traditional rhyme)

One little elephant went out to play,

Out on a spider's web one day.

It had such enormous fun,

It called for another little elephant to come.

Two little elephants went out to play,

Out on a spider's web one day.

They had such enormous fun,

They called for another little elephant to come.

Note: Continue adding elephants with each verse.

Five Little Puppies

Purpose: To practice counting

Areas of development: Logical/mathematical, oral language, written language

Materials needed: Chart paper (optional) or overhead transparency (optional), index cards or number cards

1. If you want children to follow along with the written text, copy the traditional rhyme "Five Little Puppies" (page 125) onto chart paper or duplicate it on an overhead transparency.
2. Make multiple sets of number cards with the numerals 1 through 5 or use the number cards provided on page 128. Give each child a number card to match the rhyme.
3. Have children hold up their assigned numbers when those numbers are mentioned. Note: If you think children may have difficulty understanding the ordinal numbers used in this rhyme, substitute them with natural numbers. For instance, *The first little puppy said . . .* can be substituted with *Puppy number one said . . .*

Observations

- Which children can count forward, following the counting pattern in the rhyme?
- Which children can identify their assigned numbers and connect them to the counting pattern in the rhyme?

Teacher Tip

As children connect their assigned numbers to the counting pattern in the rhyme, be sure to point out the connection between natural numbers and ordinal numbers. *Good for you, Jamie! You knew that "first" meant "one" in our rhyme.*

Five Little Puppies

(A traditional rhyme)

The first little puppy said, "Let's go out to play."

The second little puppy said, "Let's run away."

The third little puppy said, "Let's stay out till dark."

The fourth little puppy said, "Let's bark, bark, bark."

The fifth little puppy said, "I think it would be fun—

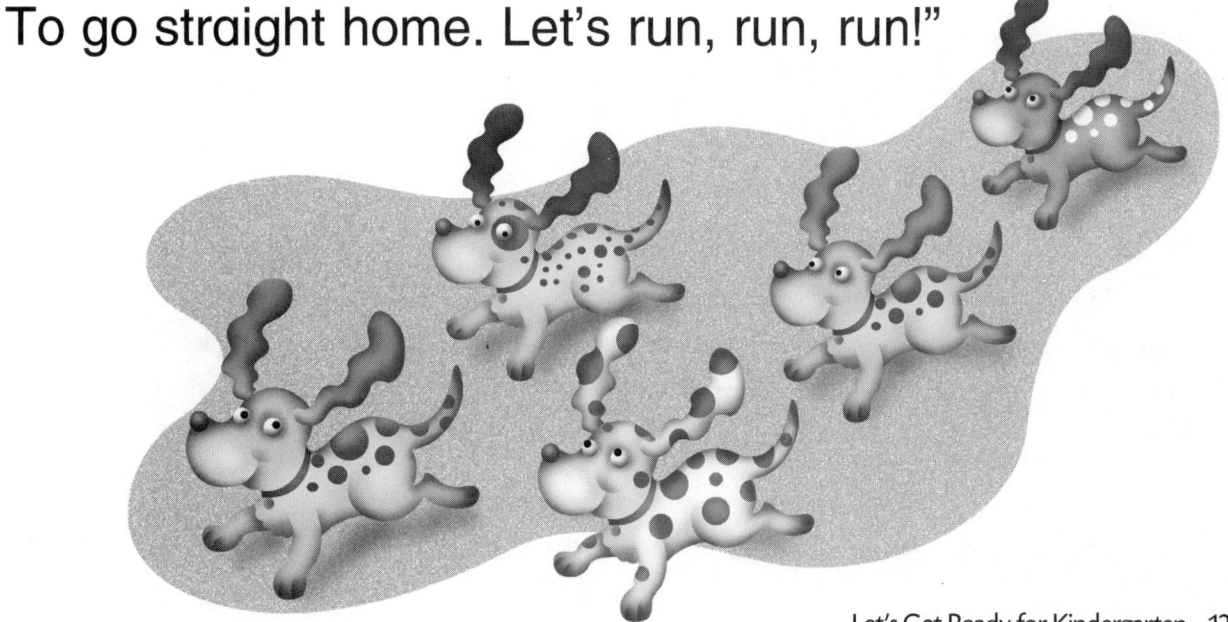

To go straight home. Let's run, run, run!"

Five Little Monkeys Jumping on the Bed

Purpose: To practice counting backward
Areas of development: Logical/mathematical, oral language, written language
Materials needed: Chart paper (optional) or overhead transparency (optional), index cards or number cards, pocket chart (optional), flannel board (optional), monkey pictures

1. If you want children to follow along with the written text, copy the traditional rhyme "Five Little Monkeys Jumping on the Bed" (page 127) onto chart paper or duplicate it on an overhead transparency.
2. Write numbers on index cards or use the number cards provided on page 128.
3. Give each child a number to match in the rhyme.
4. As you recite the rhyme with children, have them place their number in a pocket chart or on a flannel board next to the desired number of monkeys.

Observations

- Which children can identify their assigned numbers?
- Which children can count backward?

Teacher Tip

Ask for five volunteers to stand in front of the group. As you recite the rhyme, have one child sit down with each new verse. This will provide a visual for children as you count backward.

Five Little Monkeys Jumping on the Bed

(A traditional rhyme)

Five little monkeys jumping on the bed—

One fell off and bumped his head.

Momma called the doctor, and the doctor said,

"No more monkeys jumping on the bed!"

Four little monkeys jumping on the bed . . .

Note: Continue counting backward.

Number Cards

Teacher Directions:

Copy these number cards onto heavy cardstock. Cut them out and laminate them for extra durability.

1	2	3
4	5	6

Number Cards

Teacher Directions:
Copy these number cards onto heavy cardstock. Cut out and laminate them for extra durability.

7	8	9
10	11	12

Let's Get Ready for Kindergarten

Sorting This and That

Purpose: To sort items by categories
Areas of development: Logical/mathematical, oral language
Materials needed: Pictures from old magazines or sorting picture cards

Teacher Tip

For children who have difficulty sorting pictures into more than one category, spend time talking about cards that all belong in the same category. Talk about why those picture cards are all alike. Then introduce just one picture that doesn't belong and talk about why it is different.

1. Collect pictures that can be sorted into categories. You may want to laminate the pictures to make them sturdy.
2. Display five to ten pictures for children to see. Talk about each of the pictures. Encourage children to name a category for each picture. For example, *Barbara, that is an apple. You're right. That's a kind of food we eat, isn't it?*
3. Have children help you sort these pictures into groups. Tell them that the pictures in each group are similar to each other. Give an example to be sure children understand. At first, you may want to focus on one category at a time.
4. Put the picture cards into envelopes for children to sort on their own at free choice time.

Observations

- Which children can explain their reasons for sorting pictures into certain categories? For instance, can they tell you why the apple and the banana belong in the same group?
- Which children use their creativity to come up with new categories for pictures?

Ideas for Sorting Categories

- Toys
- Pets
- Animals
- Dinosaurs
- Reptiles
- Food
- Desserts
- Fruit
- Vegetables
- Letters
- High-frequency words
- Numbers
- Flowers
- Birds

- Seasonal pictures
- Seasonal clothing
- Shapes
- Colors
- Transportation
- Things to write with
- Things to draw with
- Things to read
- Places to live
- Circus pictures
- Sporting equipment
- Insects
- Places to play
- Outer space

Teacher Directions:
Copy these sorting cards onto heavy cardstock. Cut them out and laminate them for extra durability.

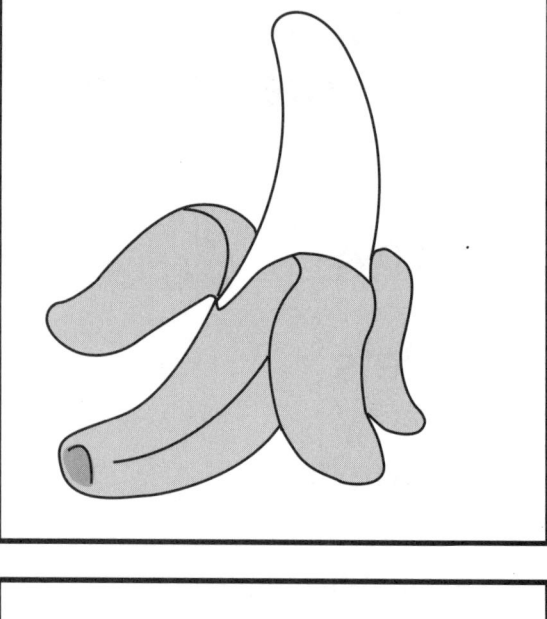

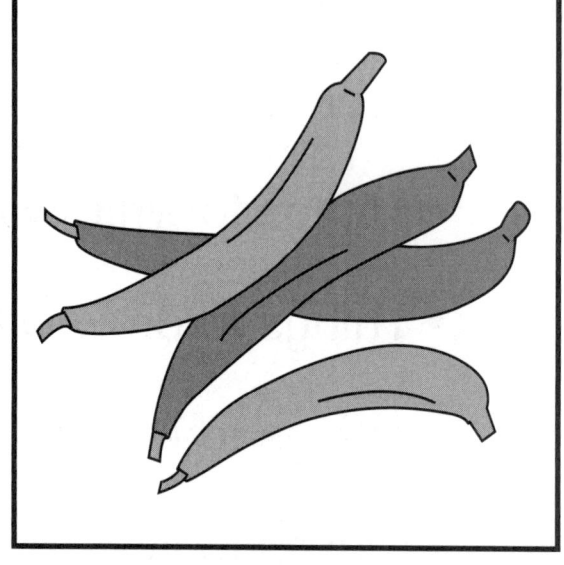

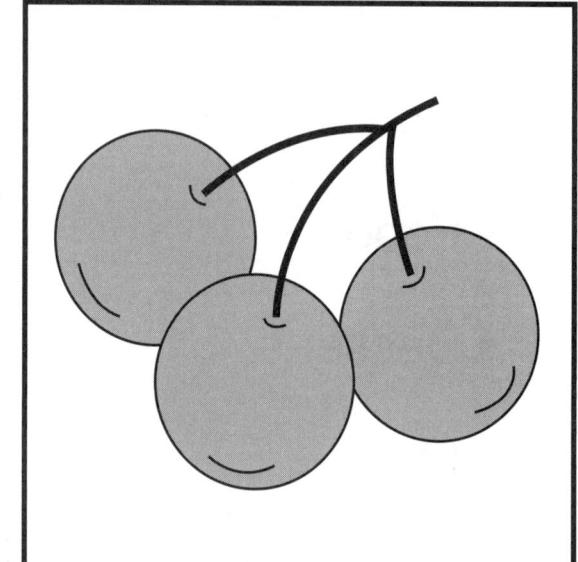

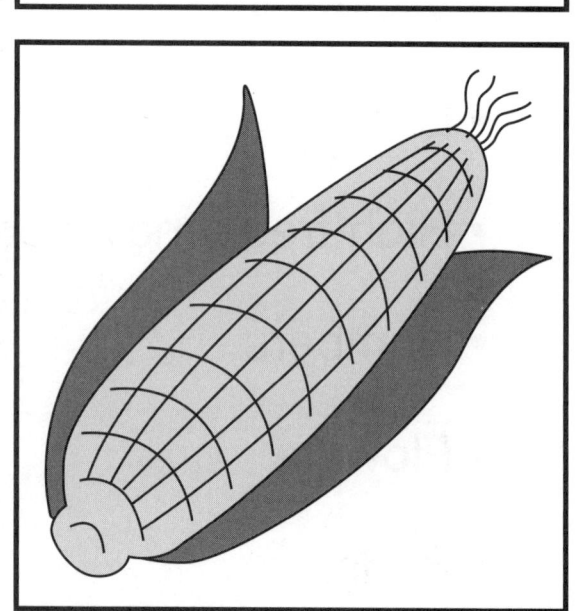

Sorting Card Set 1

132 Rigby Best Teachers Press

© 2002 Rigby

Sorting Card Set 2

Teacher Directions:

Copy these sorting cards onto heavy cardstock. Cut them out and laminate them for extra durability.

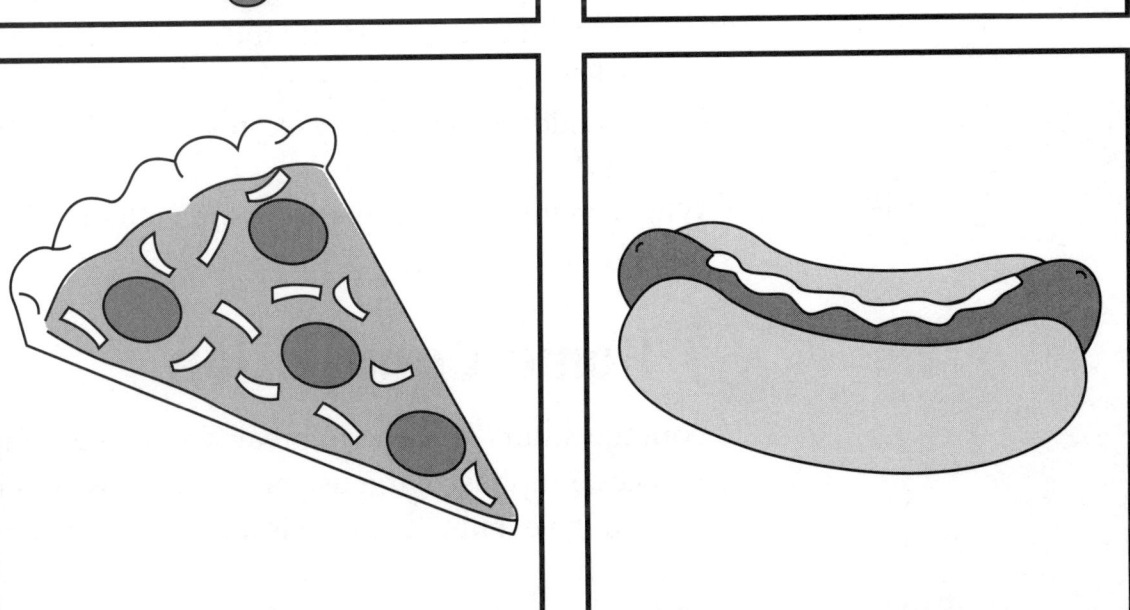

Let's Get Ready for Kindergarten 133

First, Next, Last

Purpose: To develop the ability to sequence
Areas of development: Logical/mathematical, oral language
Materials needed: Sequence cards

1. Create a set of sequence cards as shown on pages 135-137.
2. Display a set of sequence cards for children to see. Begin with a set that has only three cards. As children improve their sequencing abilities, use four and five card sets.
3. Talk with children about each of the pictures displayed. As they talk about the pictures, reinforce children's understandings by repeating back to them what they said. For instance, *Yes, Virginia, the lady is pouring the milk.*
4. Have children help you put the pictures in order. *Which of these pictures shows what happens first? What happens next?* Use sequence words like *first, second, third, next, then, last*.

Teacher Tip

If children have difficulty deciding on the sequence of an event, act out or role-play that event.

Observations

- Which children demonstrate the ability to sequence three cards? Four cards? Five cards?
- Which children can clearly express their thoughts about the pictures?
- Which children use sequence words when talking about the order of the pictures?

Home Connection

Encourage adults at home to break down everyday events into sequences. Emphasize the use of sequence words in the talk that goes with the events. Cooking is a great way to share sequencing with children.

Sequencing Card Set #1

Teacher Directions:

Copy these sequence cards onto heavy cardstock. Cut them out and laminate them for extra durability.

Let's Get Ready for Kindergarten

Sequencing Card Set 2

Teacher Directions:

Copy these sequence cards onto heavy cardstock. Cut them out and laminate them for extra durability.

136 Rigby Best Teachers Press

© 2002 Rigby

Sequencing Card Set 3

Teacher Directions:

Copy these sequence cards onto cardstock. Cut them out and laminate them for extra durability.

Let's Get Ready for Kindergarten

A Class Time Line

Purpose: To help children understand the passage of time and sequencing

Areas of development: Logical/mathematical, oral language, written language, social/emotional

Materials needed: 9-12 pieces of tag board, photos from class events, adhesive, markers

1. Create a class time line and display at eye level for children. Assign each piece of tag board to one month in the school year. Hang these monthly posters up, even those that are blank.
2. Each month take a few pictures of events that happen in the classroom. Adhere these pictures to the monthly posters. Label each event.
3. As the months pass, talk about when different events happened in the classroom. Ask: *Do you remember the first day of school? How many months ago was that now? Let's count. What happened last month? Did we pick pumpkins or plant flowers first? I wonder what might happen next month.*

Observations

- Which children understand the concept of time?
- Which children eagerly join in discussions about class events?

Teacher Tip

Make individual yearbooks for children. Each month of the school year, take pictures of important classroom events. Be sure to include their birthday celebrations at school. Then make copies of these pictures for each child and place them in their yearbooks. Children can read these books on their own over and over. They make a great end of the year gift, too. For a sample yearbook page, refer to pages 139-150, *A Year in the Life of...*

A Year in the Life of . . .

January

Look what happened!

A Year in the Life of . . .

February

Look what happened!

A Year in the Life of . . .

March

Look what happened!

A Year in the Life of . . .

April

Look what happened!

A Year in the Life of . . .

May

Look what happened!

A Year in the Life of . . .

June

Look what happened!

A Year in the Life of . . .

July

Look what happened!

A Year in the Life of . . .

August

Look what happened!

A Year in the Life of . . .

September

Look what happened!

A Year in the Life of . . .

October

Look what happened!

A Year in the Life of . . .

November

Look what happened!

A Year in the Life of . . .

December

Look what happened!

Where in the World?

Purpose: To develop understandings of spatial terms
Areas of development: Logical/mathematical, oral language
Materials needed: Bath or beach towel for each child or pair of children

1. Hand out bath or beach towels, one for at least every two children in your class. (This activity can also be done in small groups if you don't have enough towels for each pair.)
2. With the towel, model for children what it means to be:
    - Under the towel.
    - Above/over/on top of the towel.
    - Behind the towel.
    - Beside/next to the towel.
    - In front of the towel.
3. Tell children to listen closely to your directions. Then direct children to mimic the positions you just demonstrated. As children show an understanding of the spatial terms, you may want to play Simon Says with the towels.

Teacher Tip

Ask for volunteers to demonstrate spatial concepts. Be sure to praise children for their efforts, correct or incorrect. *Sam, that was nearly right. You stood behind your towel instead of beside it. Let's move you over here. Now you are standing beside your towel.*

Observations

- Which children demonstrate an understanding of spatial terms?

Home Connection

Encourage adults at home to work spatial terms into everyday discussions and tasks. For instance, when setting the table, they can direct children to place the napkins beside the plates or place the bowls on top of the plates.

Left and Right with the Hokey Pokey

Purpose: To practice left and right concepts
Areas of development: Logical/mathematical, oral language
Materials needed: None

1. Help children identify their right hands and their left hands. Tie a red ribbon around their right hands so they can differentiate between right and left as they do the Hokey Pokey. Hint: Tell children that their left thumb and first finger make an L. This is an easy way for children to differentiate between left and right.
2. Teach children the traditional song "The Hokey Pokey." (See page 153). The first or second time you sing the song, do not emphasize which arm, foot, and so on, children are to put in. Instead of singing *Put your right foot in,* sing *Put one foot in.*
3. After you have sung the song several times, then designate which arm, foot, and so on, children are to put in. Allow children approximations as they develop the right/left concept.

Observations

- Which children can easily differentiate between right and left?
- Which children look to peers to help them differentiate between right and left?
- Which children use the hint–left thumb and first finger make an L– to help them find their left hand?

Teacher Tip

Whenever you sit in a circle, for games or sharing time, use the terms right and left to help children develop understandings of this concept. For example say, *turn to the friend on the left and tell them one thing you ate for dinner last night.*

The Hokey Pokey

(A traditional song)

Put your right foot in.

Put your right foot out.

Put your right foot in and shake it all about.

Now do the Hokey Pokey

And turn yourself around.

That's what it's all about.

CLAP!

Other verses:
- Left foot
- Right arm
- Left arm
- Right hip
- Left hip
- Left leg
- Right elbow
- Left elbow
- Head
- Back end
- Right leg

Parent Activities

Dear Parents and Guardians,

Although your child spends a significant part of his or her day with me at school, you are the most important teacher your child will have! With that in mind, I will occasionally send ideas, games, and activities for you and your child to enjoy together at home. These activities will promote development in the following areas: social/emotional, fine motor, large motor, oral language, written language, and mathematical/logical.

As the year progresses and we work together to prepare your child for kindergarten, I encourage you to incorporate these activities into your weekly schedule. Your child will benefit from both the lessons learned and the quality time spent with you.

In the upper right hand corner of each activity card you will find this symbol . It is a reminder that this is an at-home activity. Each activity has a brief description and tells you the development areas it addresses. Many of these activities overlap developmental areas.

Thank you for the time and effort you give to your child as he or she prepares for kindergarten.

Sincerely,

Game Night

Set aside a night each week to play board games or card games with your child. Not only will you have fun, but you will also teach your child how to take turns, how to be a good winner and a good loser, and, in many games, how to count.

Areas of development: Social/emotional, mathematical/logical

• •

Game Night

Set aside a night each week to play board games or card games with your child. Not only will you have fun, but you will also teach your child how to take turns, how to be a good winner and a good loser, and, in many games, how to count.

Areas of development: Social/emotional, mathematical/logical

Take a Peek

Look through photo albums or magazines with your child. Talk about the facial expressions of people in the pictures. Are they happy? Sad? Angry? Surprised? Talk about the feelings people have in different situations. Encourage your child to share times when he or she felt like the people in the pictures.

Areas of development: Social/emotional, oral language

• •

Take a Peek

Look through photo albums or magazines with your child. Talk about the facial expressions of people in the pictures. Are they happy? Sad? Angry? Surprised? Talk about the feelings people have in different situations. Encourage your child to share times when he or she felt like the people in the pictures.

Areas of development: Social/emotional, oral language

Lend a Helping Hand

Begin teaching your child about taking responsibility by asking him or her to complete several simple chores on a daily or weekly basis. Chores can be as simple as watering a plant, feeding the family pet, or helping to match socks from the laundry.

Areas of development: Social/emotional, mathematical/logical

• •

Lend a Helping Hand

Begin teaching your child about taking responsibility by asking him or her to complete several simple chores on a daily or weekly basis. Chores can be as simple as watering a plant, feeding the family pet, or helping to match socks from the laundry.

Areas of development: Social/emotional, mathematical/logical

Catch It!

Play a game of catch with your child. Toss a beanbag, a tennis ball, a giant rubber ball, or even a balled up pair of clean socks. Throwing and catching activities help build muscles and hand-eye coordination, not to mention, it's fun!

Areas of development: Social/emotional, large motor

• •

Catch It!

Play a game of catch with your child. Toss a beanbag, a tennis ball, a giant rubber ball, or even a balled up pair of clean socks. Throwing and catching activities help build muscles and hand-eye coordination, not to mention, it's fun!

Areas of development: Social/emotional, large motor

Let's Go Play in the Park

Take time out of your busy schedule to enjoy some fresh air with your child. Encourage your child to pump his or her legs on the swings, to climb the ladder up the slide, and to walk on the balance beam at the local park. These activities may bring back your childhood memories while helping your child develop his or her large motor skills.

Areas of development: Social/emotional, large motor

• •

Let's Go Play in the Park

Take time out of your busy schedule to enjoy some fresh air with your child. Encourage your child to pump his or her legs on the swings, to climb the ladder up the slide, and to walk on the balance beam at the local park. These activities may bring back your childhood memories while helping your child develop his or her large motor skills.

Areas of development: Social/emotional, large motor

Sorting This Way and That

Gather a variety of small objects, such as pennies, beads, buttons, and beans. Ask your child to sort the objects in a variety of ways. Challenge your child to come up with his or her own method of sorting. Extend sorting activities by encouraging your child to count the objects that were sorted.

Areas of development: Mathematical/logical, fine motor, oral language

• •

Sorting This Way and That

Gather a variety of small objects, such as pennies, beads, buttons, and beans. Ask your child to sort the objects in a variety of ways. Challenge your child to come up with his or her own method of sorting. Extend sorting activities by encouraging your child to count the objects that were sorted.

Areas of development: Mathematical/logical, fine motor, oral language

An Artist at Work

Encourage your child's artistic talents by providing a variety of painting opportunities. Paint-by-number, finger painting, and painting with watercolors are all activities that will build your child's fine motor skills along with his or her artistic expression. Be sure to ask your child about his or her artwork. You might even write a caption or story to go with the painting.

Areas of development: Fine motor, social/emotional, oral language

• •

An Artist at Work

Encourage your child's artistic talents by providing a variety of painting opportunities. Paint-by-number, finger painting, and painting with watercolors are all activities that will build your child's fine motor skills along with his or her artistic expression. Be sure to ask your child about his or her artwork. You might even write a caption or story to go with the painting.

Areas of development: Fine motor, social/emotional, oral language

Take notes

Fill a basket with writing supplies including pencils, pens, markers, crayons, paper, stationary, and envelopes. Encourage your child to write on a daily basis. With the use of a small spiral notebook and a pencil, your child can help you write the grocery list, write notes to family members, and write about the day's events. Their pictures, letters, and sometimes illegible text is writing. What is important to remember is that your child is writing and expressing his or her thoughts. Invite your child to read his or her writing to you. Focus on the story your child tells rather than the actual correctness of the written work.

Areas of development: Written language, fine motor, oral language

• •

Take notes

Fill a basket with writing supplies including pencils, pens, markers, crayons, paper, stationary, and envelopes. Encourage your child to write on a daily basis. With the use of a small spiral notebook and a pencil, your child can help you write the grocery list, write notes to family members, and write about the day's events. Their pictures, letters, and sometimes illegible text is writing. What is important to remember is that your child is writing and expressing his or her thoughts. Invite your child to read his or her writing to you. Focus on the story your child tells rather than the actual correctness of the written work.

Areas of development: Written language, fine motor, oral language

My Own ABC Book

Create an ABC book with your child. Using a notebook, a small photo album, or even paper stapled together, gather pictures to put into an ABC book. Together, take photographs of objects beginning with each letter of the alphabet or find pictures in magazines to include. Invite your child to help you cut out and glue pictures to the appropriate pages. Be sure to label each page using both uppercase and lowercase letters. As your child reads his or her ABC book to you, encourage him or her to point to each object on a page.

Areas of development: Written language, fine motor, oral language, social/emotional

• •

My Own ABC Book

Create an ABC book with your child. Using a notebook, a small photo album, or even paper stapled together, gather pictures to put into an ABC book. Together, take photographs of objects beginning with each letter of the alphabet or find pictures in magazines to include. Invite your child to help you cut out and glue pictures to the appropriate pages. Be sure to label each page using both uppercase and lowercase letters. As your child reads his or her ABC book to you, encourage him or her to point to each object on a page.

Areas of development: Written language, fine motor, oral language, social/emotional

Say That Again

Play an echo game with your child. Tell him or her that you will say something and that he or she should repeat what you say. Children love to play this game, especially if you add some rhythm, rhyme, and silliness to what you say. For example: *Oh me! Oh my!* (Echo) *Today I saw a fly!* (Echo) *He flew up in a tree.* (Echo) *And then he winked at me.* (Echo)

Areas of development: Oral language, social/emotional

• •

Say That Again

Play an echo game with your child. Tell him or her that you will say something and that he or she should repeat what you say. Children love to play this game, especially if you add some rhythm, rhyme, and silliness to what you say. For example: *Oh me! Oh my!* (Echo) *Today I saw a fly!* (Echo) *He flew up in a tree.* (Echo) *And then he winked at me.* (Echo)

Areas of development: Oral language, social/emotional

Word Webs

Word Webs are a great way to build your child's vocabulary. They can be done quickly and can pass the time in the car, while waiting at the doctor's office, or while you make dinner. Tell your child that together you will think of as many words as you can that go with a chosen word. For example: *Let's think of words that go with "happy."* Choose other feeling words or categories, such as colors, fruits, breakfast foods, things that make you laugh.

Areas of development: Oral language, social/emotional

• •

Word Webs

Word Webs are a great way to build your child's vocabulary. They can be done quickly and can pass the time in the car, while waiting at the doctor's office, or while you make dinner. Tell your child that together you will think of as many words as you can that go with a chosen word. For example: *Let's think of words that go with "happy."* Choose other feeling words or categories, such as colors, fruits, breakfast foods, things that make you laugh.

Areas of development: Oral language, social/emotional

Rhyming Riddles

Helping your child to understand the concept of rhyming is important as he or she develops oral language and written language skills. Begin reciting a familiar nursery rhyme. After saying the first part of the rhyme, leave out the next rhyming part and ask your child to fill in the blank. For example: *Jack and Jill went up the ____ to fetch a pail of water. Jack fell down and broke his____ and Jill came tumbling after.*

Areas of development: Oral language

• •

Rhyming Riddles

Helping your child to understand the concept of rhyming is important as he or she develops oral language and written language skills. Begin reciting a familiar nursery rhyme. After saying the first part of the rhyme, leave out the next rhyming part and ask your child to fill in the blank. For example: *Jack and Jill went up the ____ to fetch a pail of water. Jack fell down and broke his____ and Jill came tumbling after.*

Areas of development: Oral language

How Many Seeds

As you and your child enjoy a piece of fruit, invite him or her to count the number of seeds in the fruit. Make note of how many seeds were in your piece of fruit and help your child compare it with the number of seeds in his or her piece of fruit. You may also want to compare the number of seeds from each day's fruit snack.

Areas of development: Mathematical/logical

• •

How Many Seeds

As you and your child enjoy a piece of fruit, invite him or her to count the number of seeds in the fruit. Make note of how many seeds were in your piece of fruit and help your child compare it with the number of seeds in his or her piece of fruit. You may also want to compare the number of seeds from each day's fruit snack.

Areas of development: Mathematical/logical

Cooking in the Kitchen

Invite your child to help you prepare a meal. Read aloud the recipes and ask your child to help you measure the ingredients. Do not expect your child to understand the concepts of teaspoons, tablespoons, ounces, and so on. However, encourage your child to help with the measuring by saying: *We need four spoonfuls of salt*. Your child can do the counting out loud as you measure four units of salt. This will help your child understand one-to–one correspondence in addition to giving him or her practice in counting.

Areas of development: Mathematical/logical, oral language

• •

Cooking in the Kitchen

Invite your child to help you prepare a meal. Read aloud the recipes and ask your child to help you measure the ingredients. Do not expect your child to understand the concepts of teaspoons, tablespoons, ounces, and so on. However, encourage your child to help with the measuring by saying: *We need four spoonfuls of salt*. Your child can do the counting out loud as you measure four units of salt. This will help your child understand one-to–one correspondence in addition to giving him or her practice in counting.

Areas of development: Mathematical/logical, oral language

Weather Report

Create a blank calendar grid. Each day ask your child to give you a weather report. Record the weather on the calendar with simple pictures to represent the types of weather. Then once a week, invite your child to count the number of sunny, cloudy, rainy, snowy, windy, or foggy days. Ask your child questions such as: *Were there more sunny days this week or more cloudy days? What was the weather like two days ago?*

Areas of development: Mathematical/logical, oral language

• •

Weather Report

Create a blank calendar grid. Each day ask your child to give you a weather report. Record the weather on the calendar with simple pictures to represent the types of weather. Then once a week, invite your child to count the number of sunny, cloudy, rainy, snowy, windy, or foggy days. Ask your child questions such as: *Were there more sunny days this week or more cloudy days? What was the weather like two days ago?*

Areas of development: Mathematical/logical, oral language

Scope and Sequence

Activity Name; Page Number	Social/ Emotional Development	Oral Language Development	Written Language Development	Fine Motor Development	Large Motor Development	Logical/ Mathematical Development
Self-Portrait; 11	●	●				
I Have Ten Little Fingers; 12	●	●	●			●
Mary Wore a Red Dress; 14	●	●	●			
Partner Pictures; 15	●	●		●		
Pattern-Making; 16	●	●		●		●
Cooperative Play; 18	●	●				●
Role-Playing Cards; 19	●	●				
It's a Mystery!; 23		●				●
Name That; 24	●	●				
Riddle This, Riddle That; 26		●				●
What Happened Next?; 30		●				
Who? What? Where? When? Why? How?; 32	●	●				
Then What Happened?; 34		●	●			●
Mistakes; 36		●	●			
This Old Man; 38		●	●			

Let's Get Ready for Kindergarten

Activity Name; Page Number	Social/ Emotional Development	Oral Language Development	Written Language Development	Fine Motor Development	Large Motor Development	Logical/ Mathematical Development
Roses are Red; 40		●	●			
Rhyming Card Concentration; 42		●	●			●
A,B,C…Look What I Can See!; 45		●	●	●		
We Can Read Our Environment; 47		●	●	●		
Environmental Print Concentration; 48	●		●			●
My Own I Can Read Books; 50	●	●	●			
Environmental Print Hopscotch; 56			●		●	
Old MacDonald Had a Farm; 58		●	●			
Bingo; 60		●	●			
Miss Mary Mack; 62		●	●			
ABC Assessment; 68			●			
A, my name is Allison; 71	●		●	●		
Rooms for Rent; 72	●	●	●			
Name Concentration; 74	●		●			●
My Very Own Rebus Story; 75	●		●			

172 Rigby Best Teachers Press

© 2002 Rigby

Activity Name; Page Number	Social/ Emotional Development	Oral Language Development	Written Language Development	Fine Motor Development	Large Motor Development	Logical/ Mathematical Development
Color Concentration; 76						●
Writing Center; 79	●	●	●			
Concepts About Print; 83			●			
Amazing Mazes; 89				●		
Fun with Lines and Shapes; 93				●		
Highlight That!; 97	●			●		
Follow the Leader; 99	●	●			●	
Simon Says; 100	●	●			●	
Busting out with Balloons; 101	●				●	
Beanbag Toss; 102	●				●	●
Bowl Me Over!; 103	●				●	●
Obstacle Course; 104					●	
Head, Shoulders, Knees, and Toes; 106		●	●		●	
If You're Happy...; 108		●	●		●	
The Grasshopper; 110		●	●		●	

Let's Get Ready for Kindergarten 173

Activity Name; Page Number	Social/ Emotional Development	Oral Language Development	Written Language Development	Fine Motor Development	Large Motor Development	Logical/ Mathematical Development
Large Motor Center; 112	●				●	
Vital Information; 117	●					●
Over in the Meadow; 118		●	●	●		●
Hickory Dickory Dock; 120		●	●			●
Elephant Song; 122		●	●			●
Five Little Puppies; 124		●	●			●
Five Little Monkeys Jumping on the Bed; 126		●	●		●	●
Sorting This and That; 130		●				●
First, Next, Last; 134		●				●
A Class Time Line; 138	●		●			●
Where in the World?; 151		●				●
Left and Right with the Hokey Pokey; 152		●				●

174 Rigby Best Teachers Press

© 2002 Rigby

References

Cambourne, Brian. *Whole Story: Natural Learning and the Acquisition of Literacy* New York: Scholastic, 1988.

Fisher, Bobbi. *Joyful Learning.* Portsmouth, NH: Heinemann, 1991.

Holdaway, Don. *The Foundations of Literacy.* Portsmouth, NH: Heinemann, 1979.

Holley, Cynthia. *Warming Up to Big Books.* San Diego, CA: Wright Group, 1995.

Parkes, Brenda. *Read It Again!.* Portland, ME: Stenhouse Publishers, 2000.

Pebble Soup, Crystal Lake, IL: Rigby, 2000.